Queen Anne Architecture in Ontario in Colour Photos, Saving Our History One Photo at a Time

Photography
by Barbara Raué
2019

Series Name: Architectural Styles

Book 1: Queen Anne

Cover photo: Niagara Falls Book 1 - 5982 Culp Street, Page 62

All the photos in this book have been taken with my cameras. I own the rights to them.

Queen Anne, 1885-1900 – This style is distinguished by an irregular outline featuring a combination of an offset tower, broad gables, projecting two-storey bays, verandahs, multi-sloped roofs, and tall, decorative chimneys. A mixture of brick and wood is common. Windows often have one large single-paned bottom sash and small panes in the upper sash.

This book is dedicated to the Queen Anne style of architecture in Ontario with more than one hundred homes to admire.

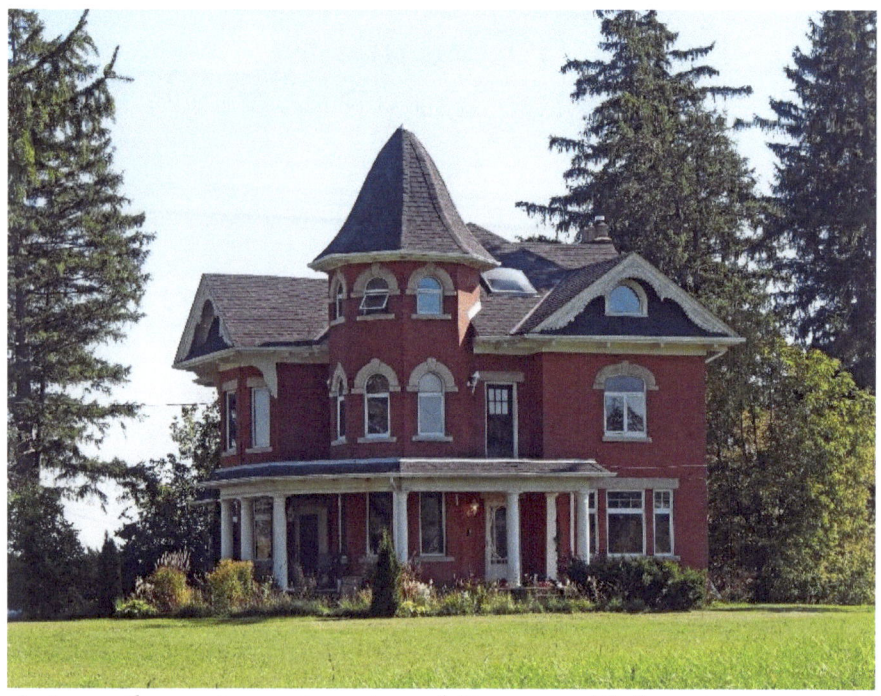

Acton - three storey turret, architraves with keystones, verge board trim on gables, fretwork, ionic pillars

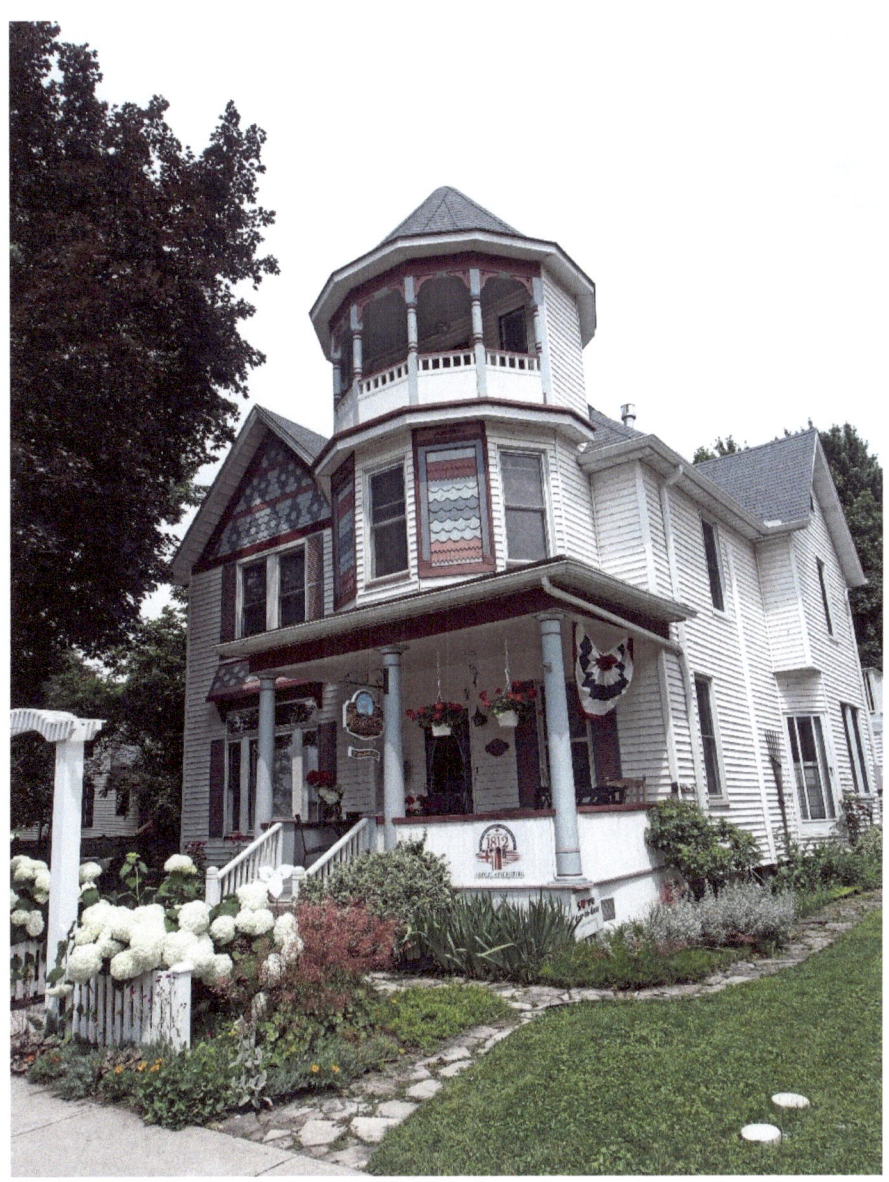

Amherstburg Book 1 - 199 Dalhousie Street – Bondy House Bed and Breakfast - Century old Victorian Queen Anne home, turret called "Widow's Walk" for a great view, trichromatic siding

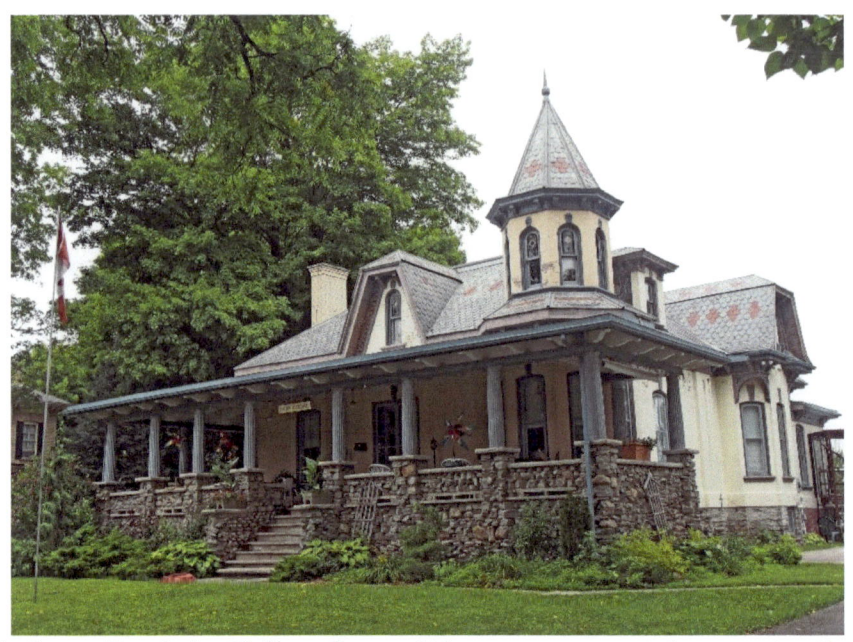
Aylmer Book 1 - Talbot Street West – turret, trichromatic tile work

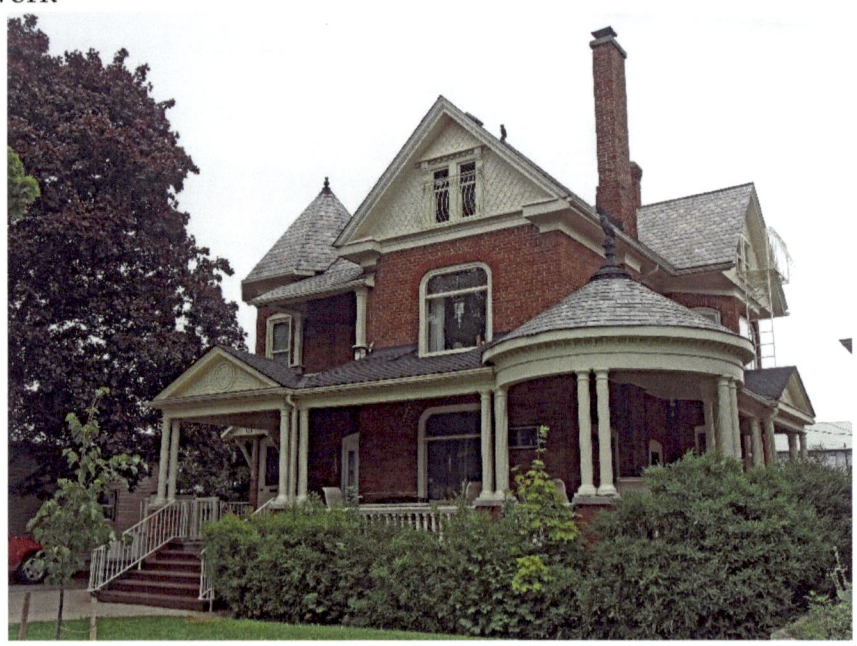
Aylmer Book 2 - 111 Sydenham Street East – turret

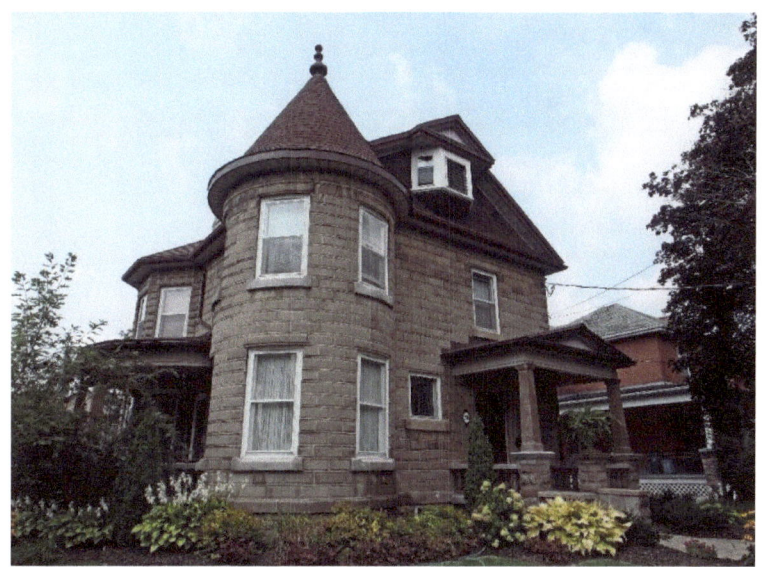

Belleville Book 1 - 278 George Street – Queen Anne style – two-storey tower with cone-shaped roof, pediment above porch, semi-circular veranda

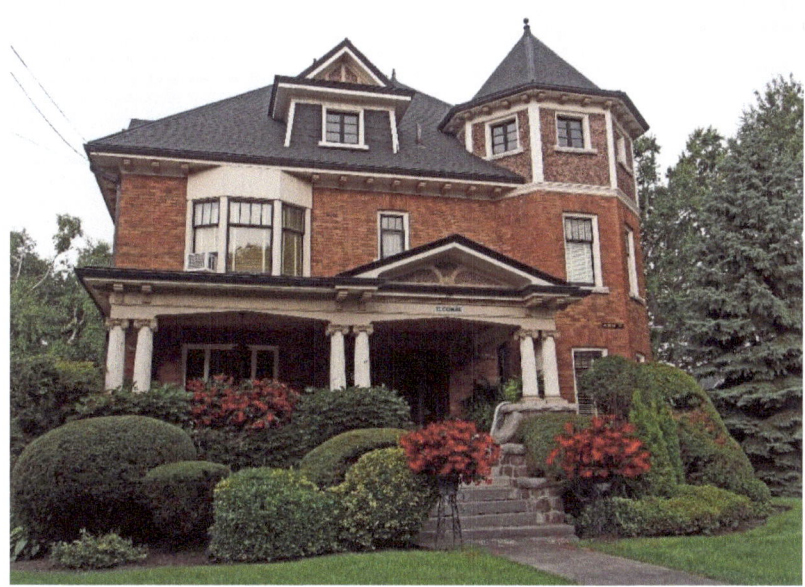

Belleville Book 2 - 234 Ann Street (corner of Queen) – Ilcombe – three-storey tower, dormer, Ionic veranda pillars

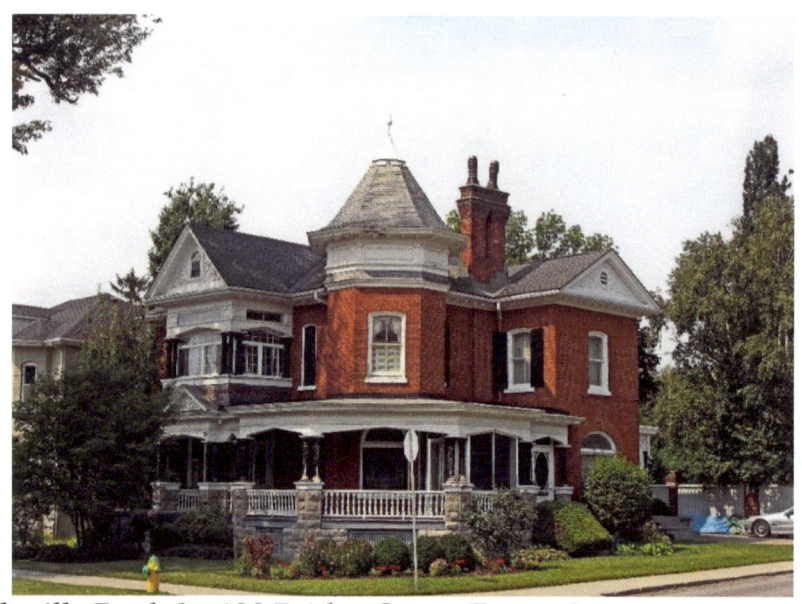

Belleville Book 3 - 128 Bridge Street East – Queen Anne style – turret, tall decorative chimney, decorative tympanums on the gables, pediment, open railing on the veranda

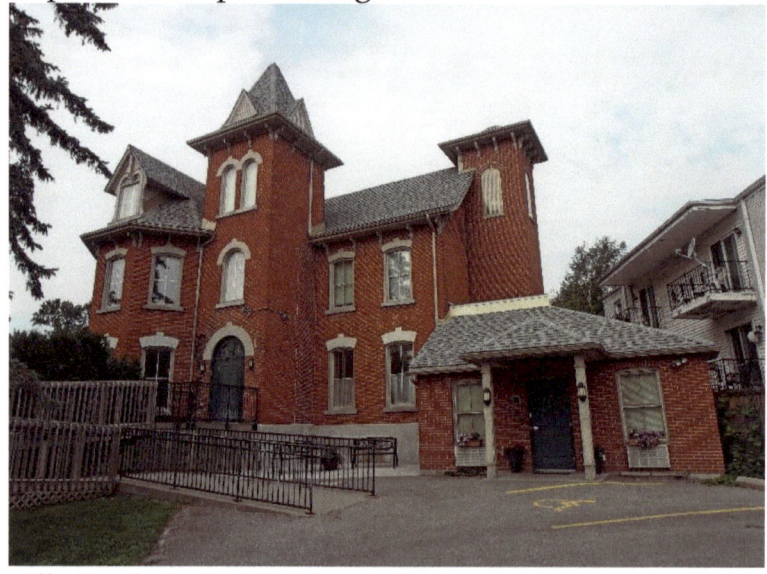

Belleville Book 4 - 58 Highland Avenue – Queen Anne style – three-storey tower, turret, cornice brackets, voussoirs and keystones

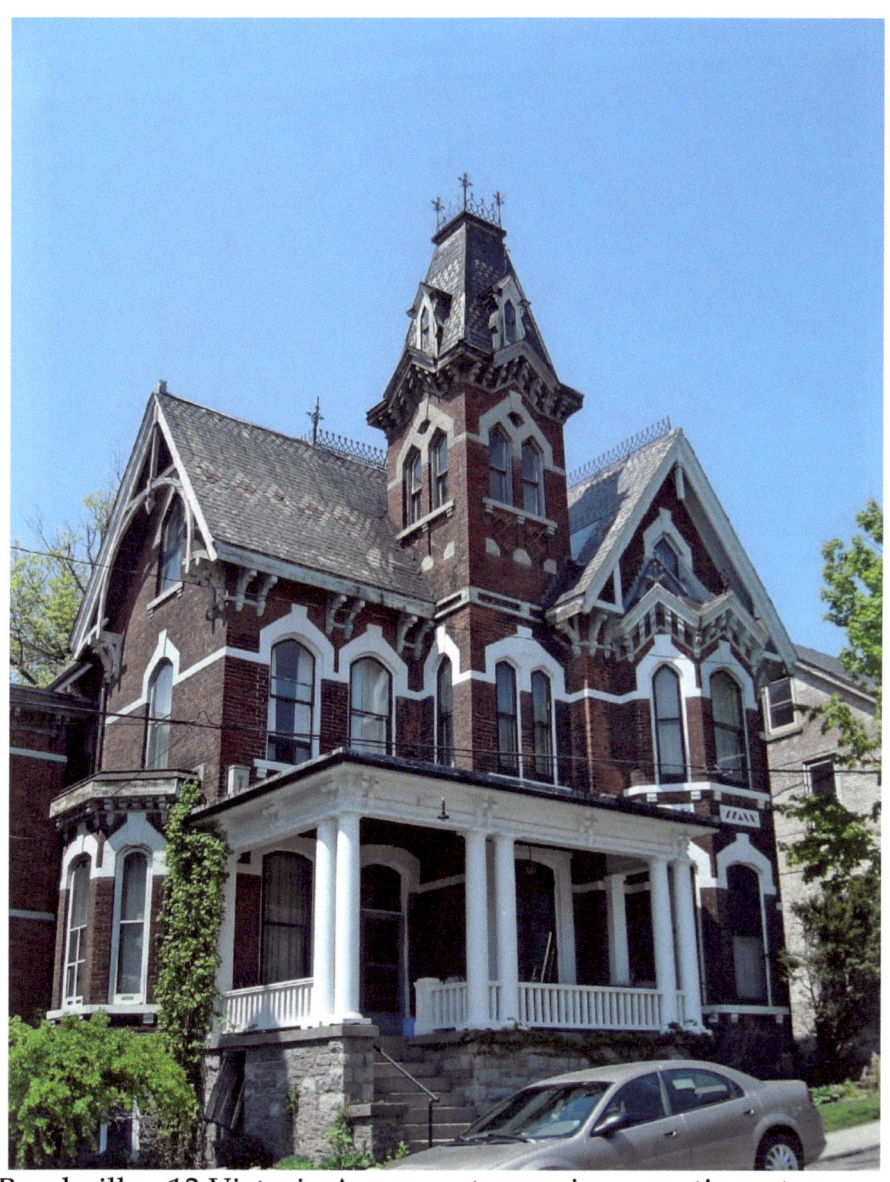

Brockville - 12 Victoria Avenue - tower, iron cresting; stone keystones and banding; verge board trim, finials; bay windows; veranda with Doric columns

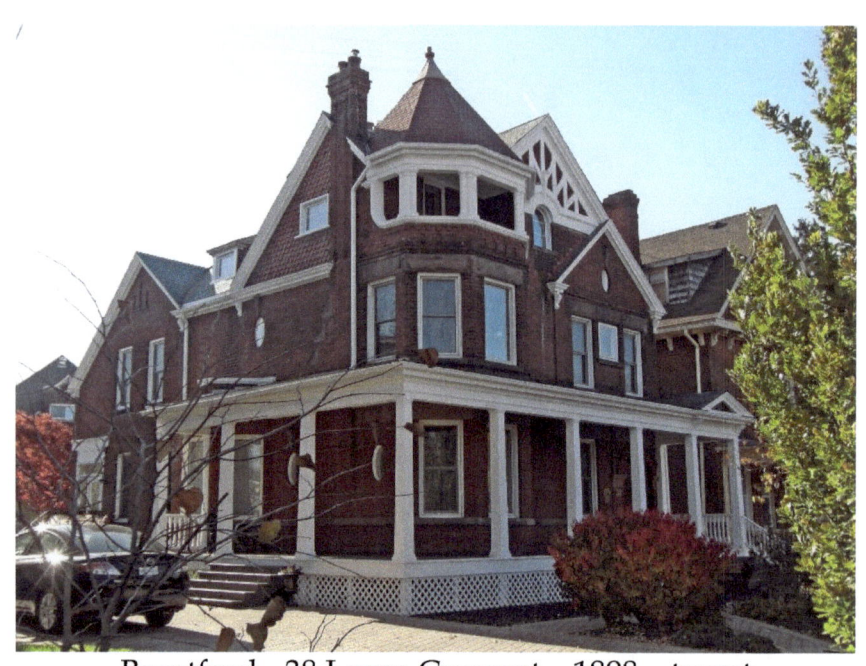
Brantford - 38 Lorne Crescent – 1898 – turret

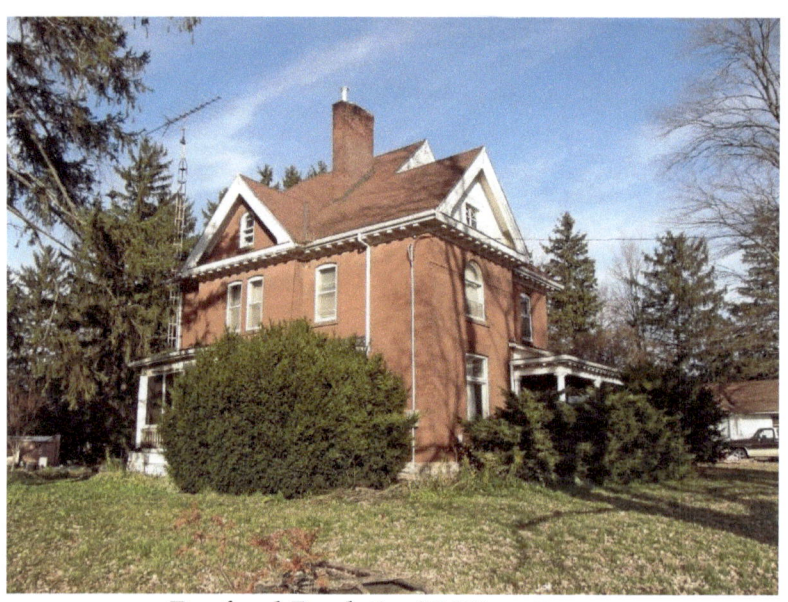
Burford Book 1 - 80 King Street

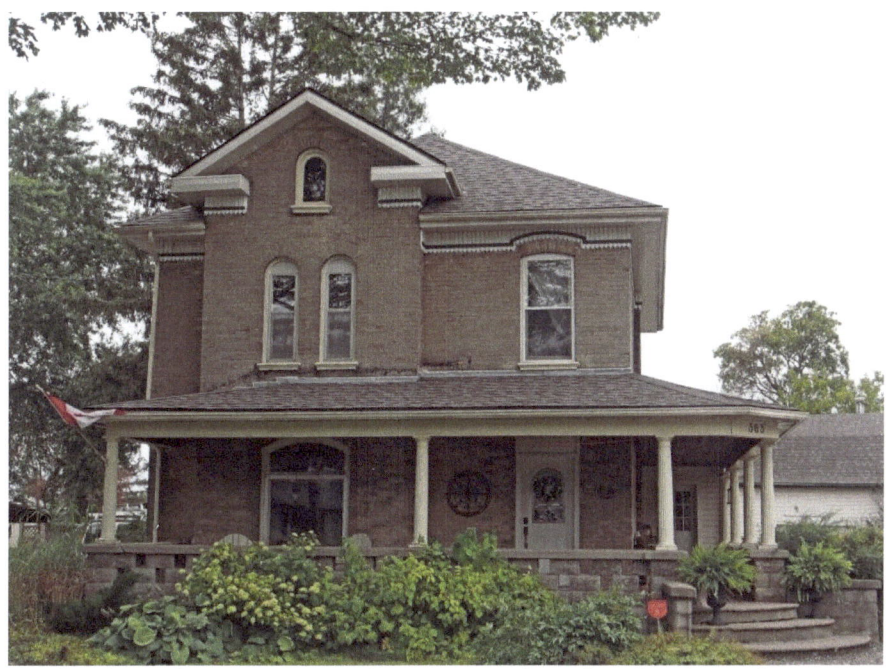

Burford Book 2 - 363 Maple Avenue South – built in the Queen Anne style by George Holt with a wraparound porch with wooden pillars. The upper storey has a bay window with one gable and cornice returns and rounded windows. There is decorative fretting under the eaves.

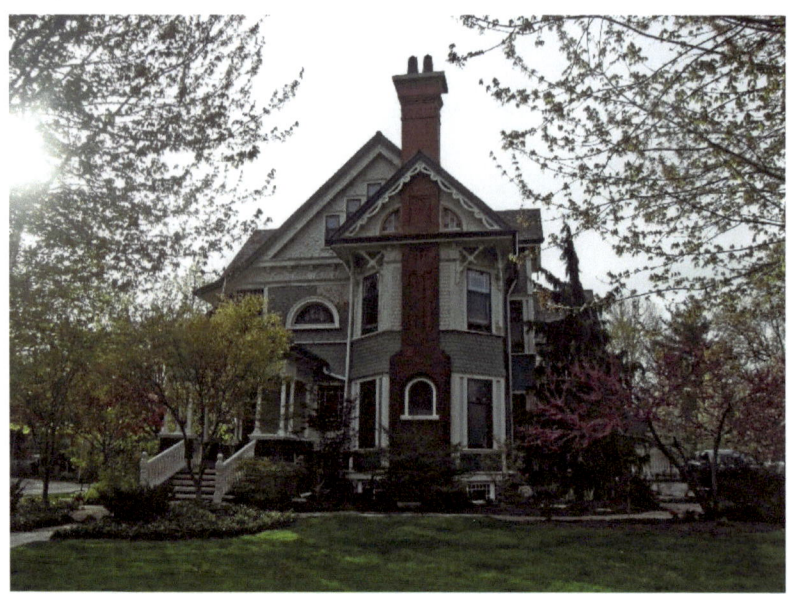

Burlington - Burlington Avenue – vergeboard trim, decorative brickwork below cornice, half-moon window, fish-scale pattern on tower

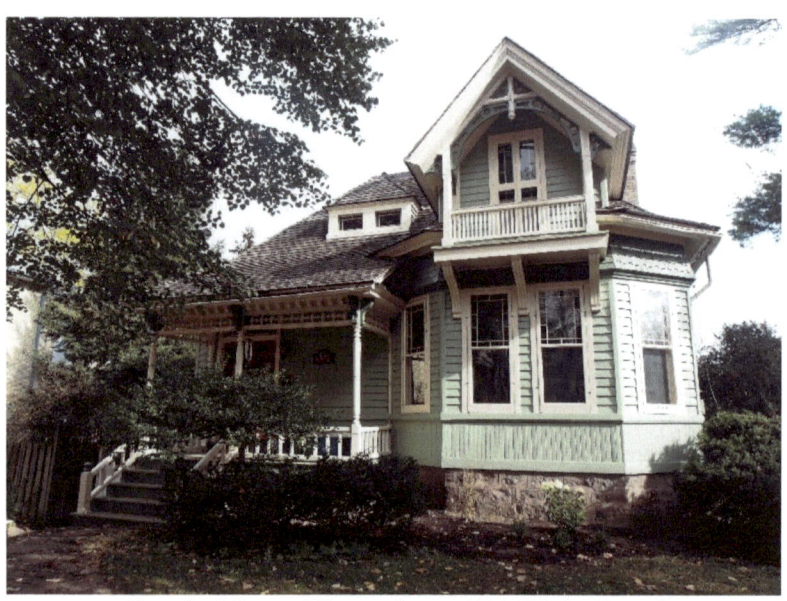

Cambridge - Hespeler - 126 Blair Road

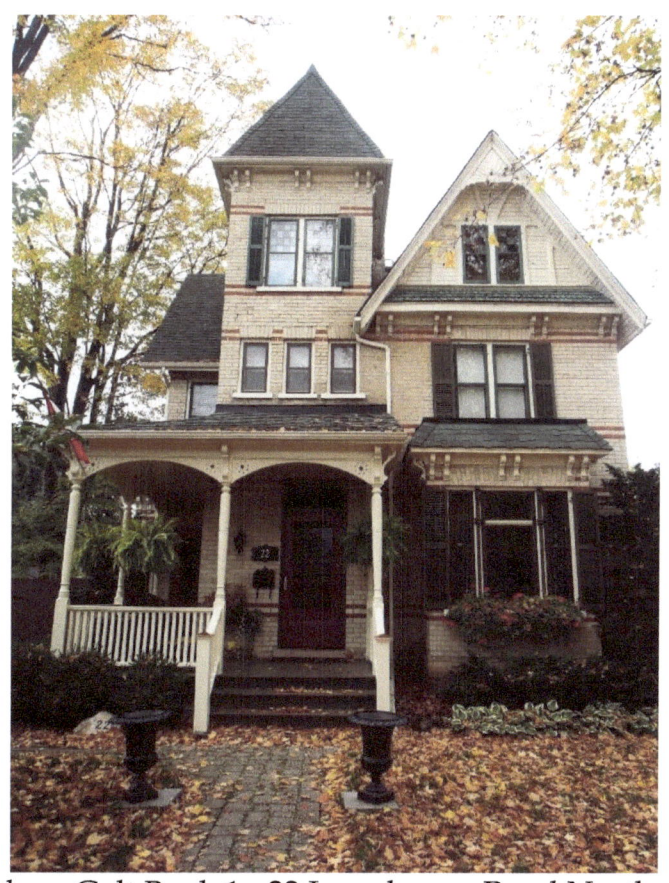

Cambridge - Galt Book 1 - 22 Lansdowne Road North – vergeboard trim on gable, dichromatic brickwork, cornice brackets on bay window

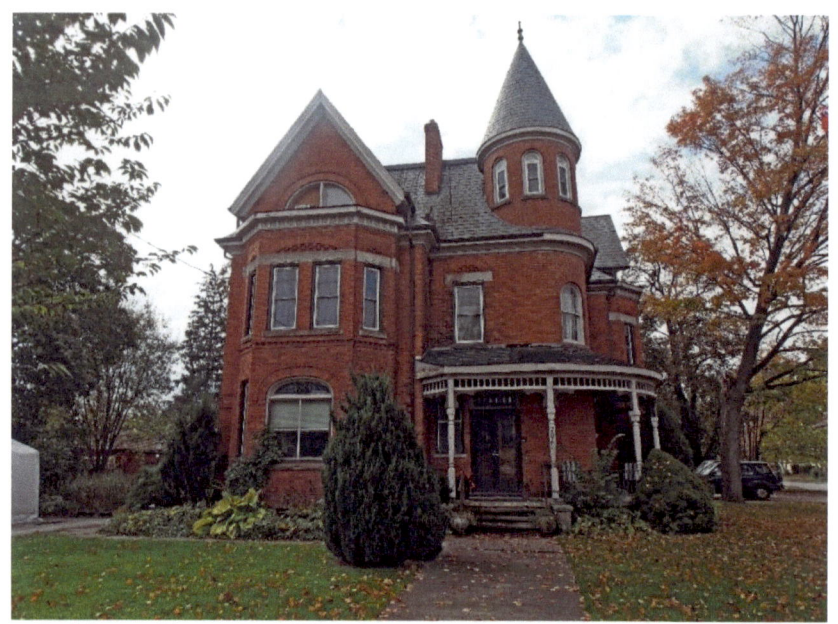

Cambridge - Preston - 706 Queenston Road - a two-and-a-half storey tower-like bay with gable, three-storey tower with cone-shaped roof

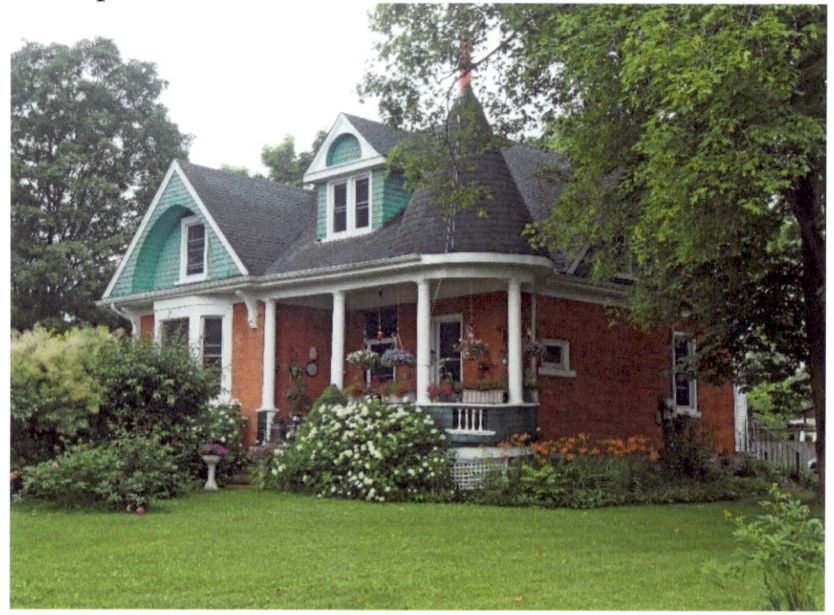

Clifford - turret, dormer, bay window

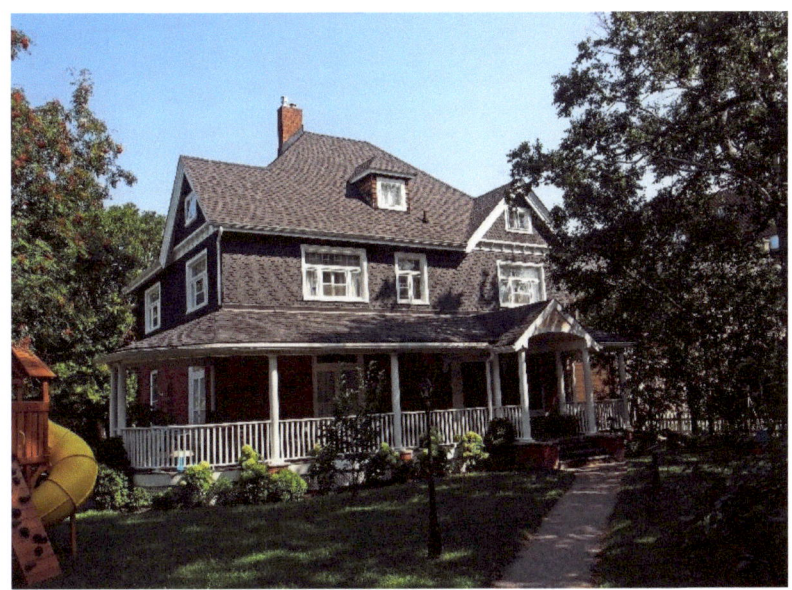

Cobourg Book 1 - 214 King Street East – c. 1891 - Home of George Armour, son of Chief Justice of Canada (John Armour), from 1910 to 1930s. Queen Anne Style with irregular plan

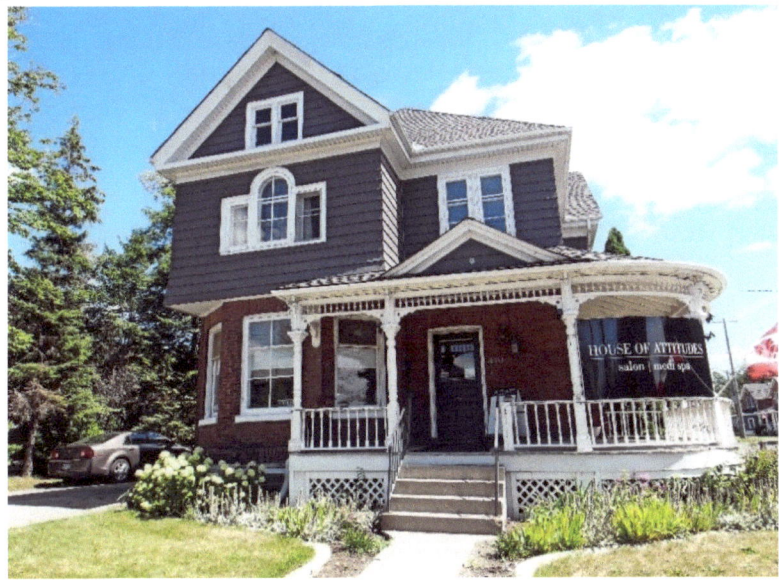

Cobourg Book 4 - 410 Division Street – 1890-1900 – George Stanton House – Queen Anne element

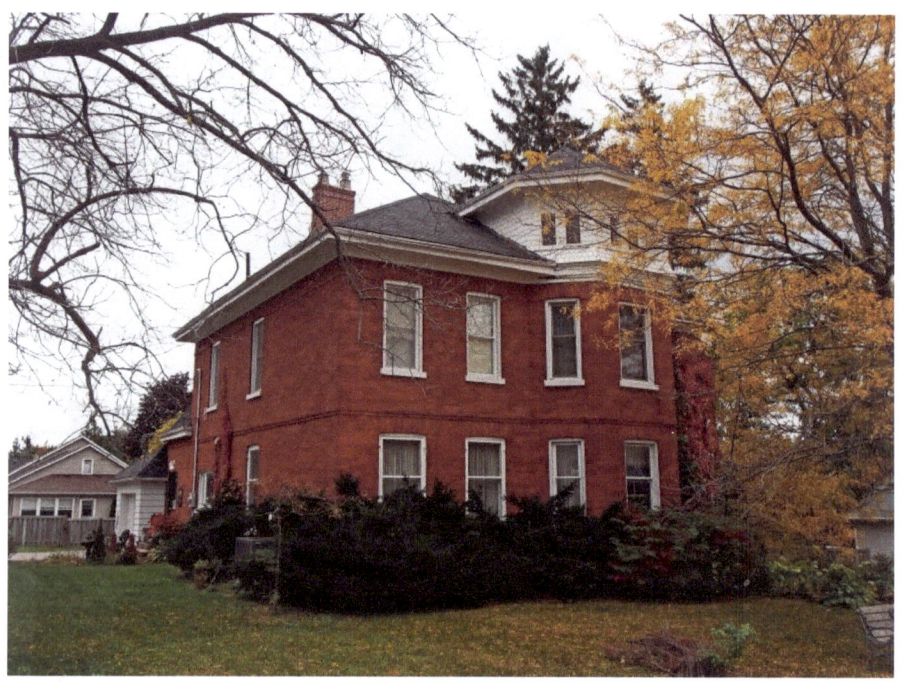

Colborne - 8 Victory Street - During the reign of Queen Anne (1702-1714) an architectural style was born and it enjoyed a revival, particularly in the New World, in the latter part of the 19th century. 8 Victory Lane (as it was then known) is a fine example of this style of architecture. It is characterized by fine brickwork in warm, soft finished tones, terracotta panels and crisply painted white woodwork.

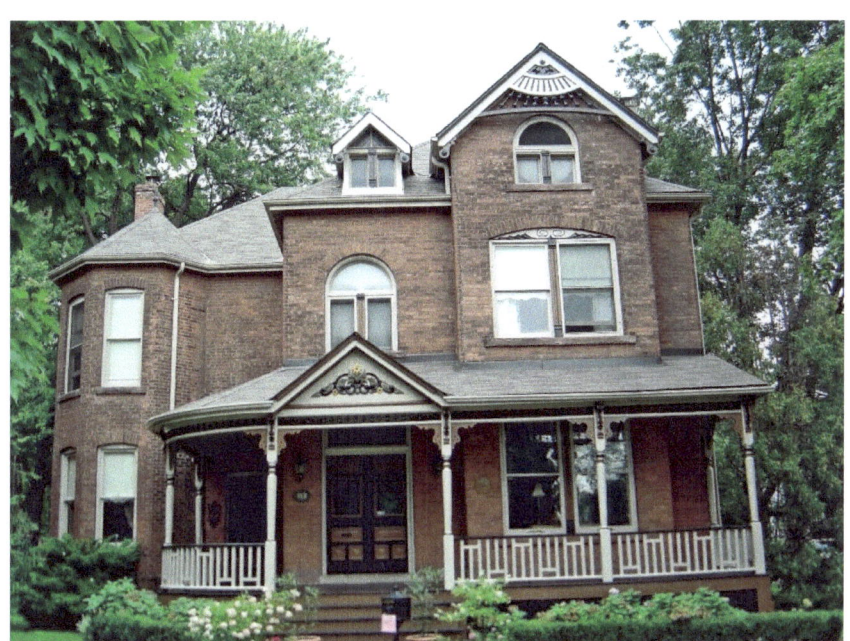
Dundas Book 3 - 113 Melville Street

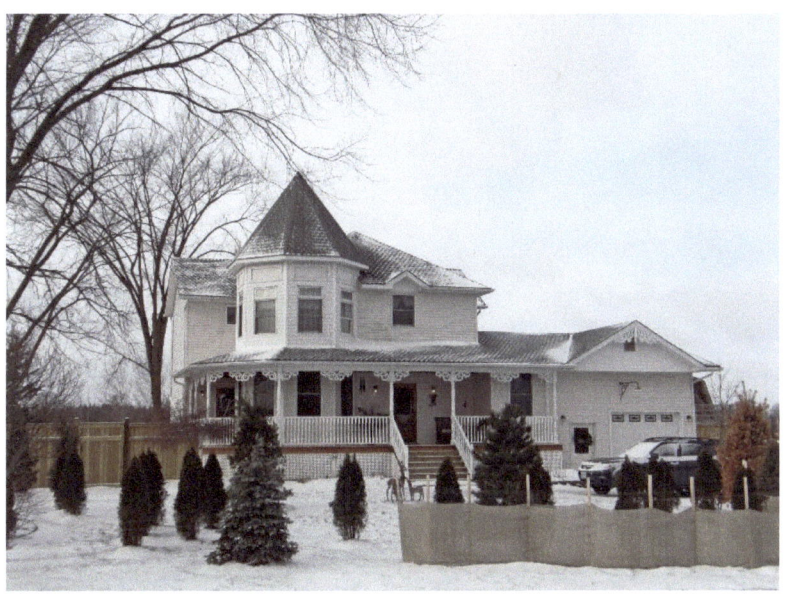
Eden Mills Book – Eramosa - - turret

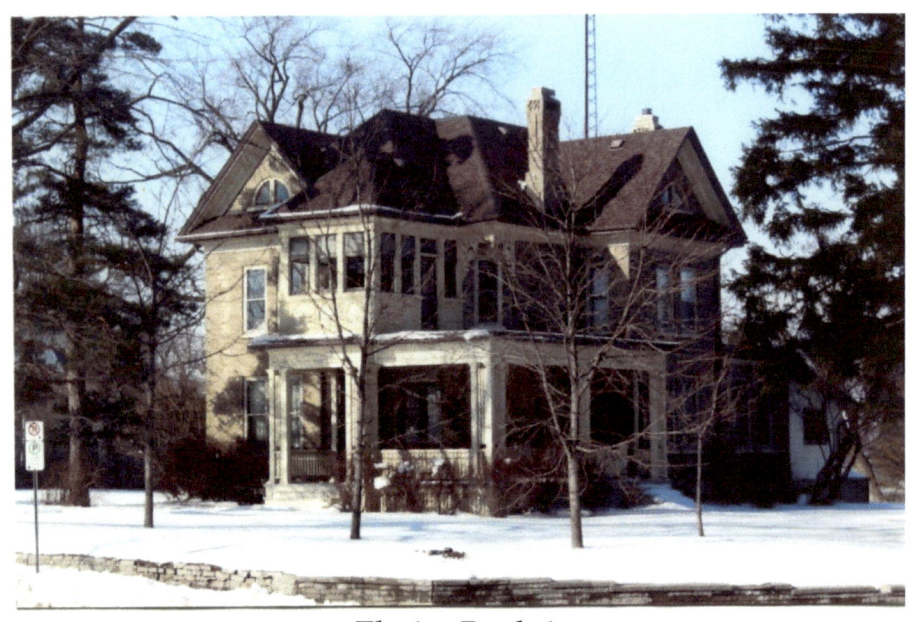

Elmira Book 1

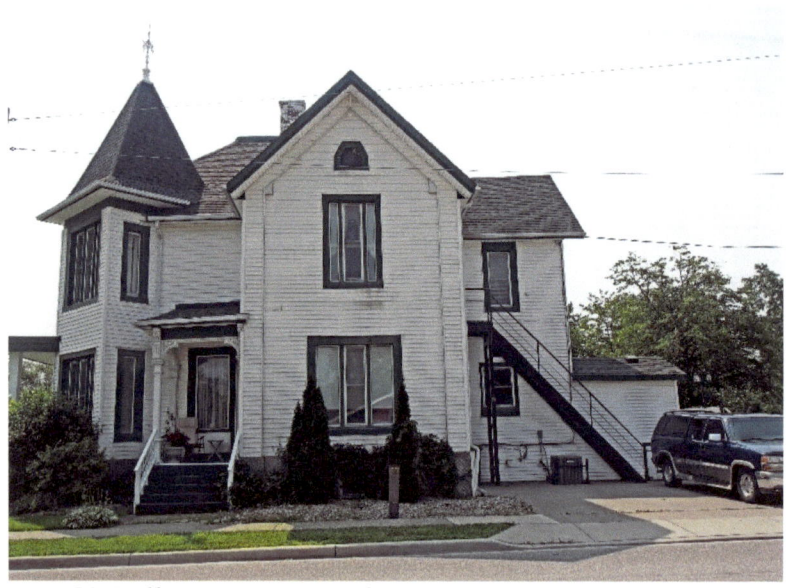

Essex - 122 Talbot Street South – Essex Manor Rest Home - two-story

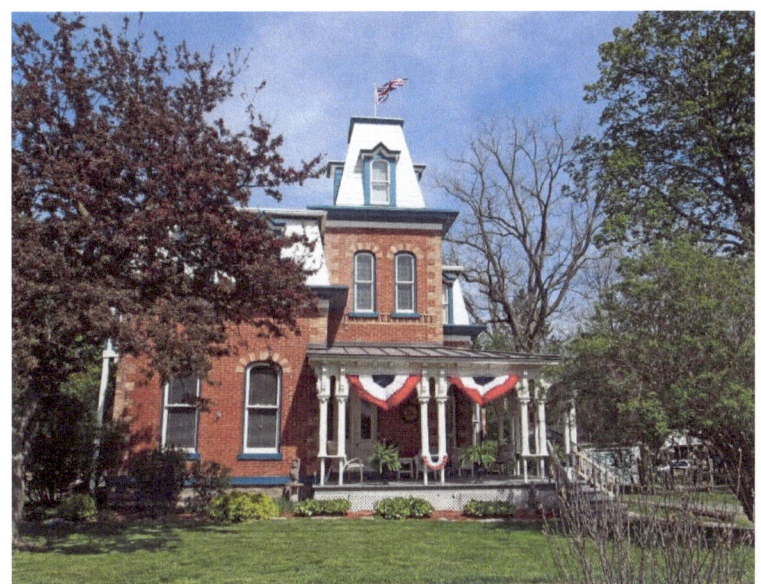

Fort Erie Book – Ridgeway - 348 Ridge Road North

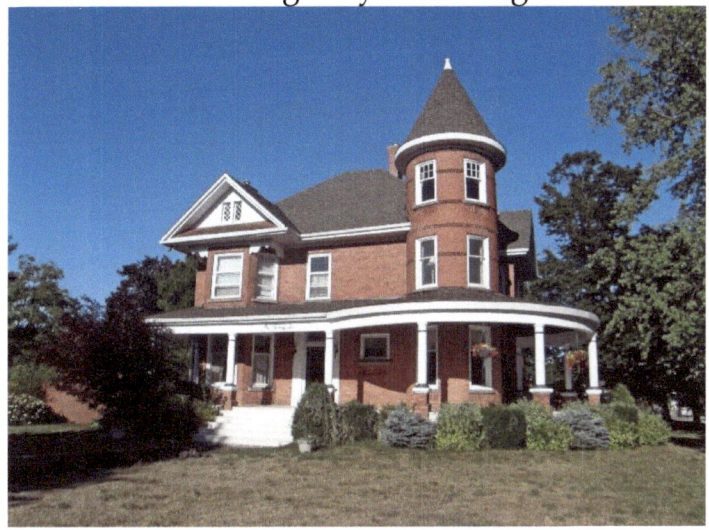

Goderich - 126 North Street, the Baechler House, was built in 1882 for druggist James Wilson, but it was in the Baechler family for 60 years. The tower with curved glass windows and the deep verandah wrapping around the building are typical of the Queen Anne style.

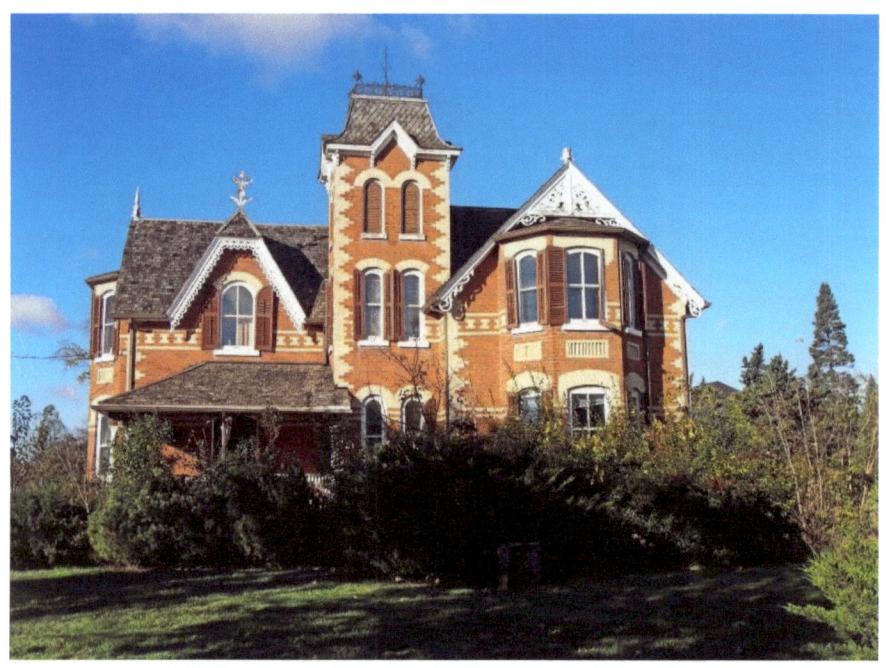

Grafton and Bolton Book - 6012 King Road, Nobleton – Hambly House – c. 1884 – It was originally built of logs but was rebuilt after a fire at the corner of Highway 27 and King Road.

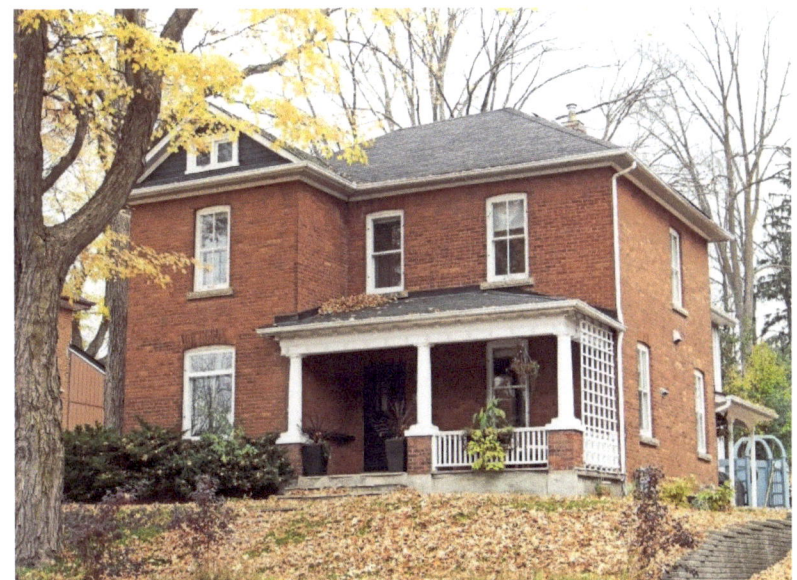

Grafton and Bolton Book - 105 King Street West, Bolton – Queen Anne style (plain)

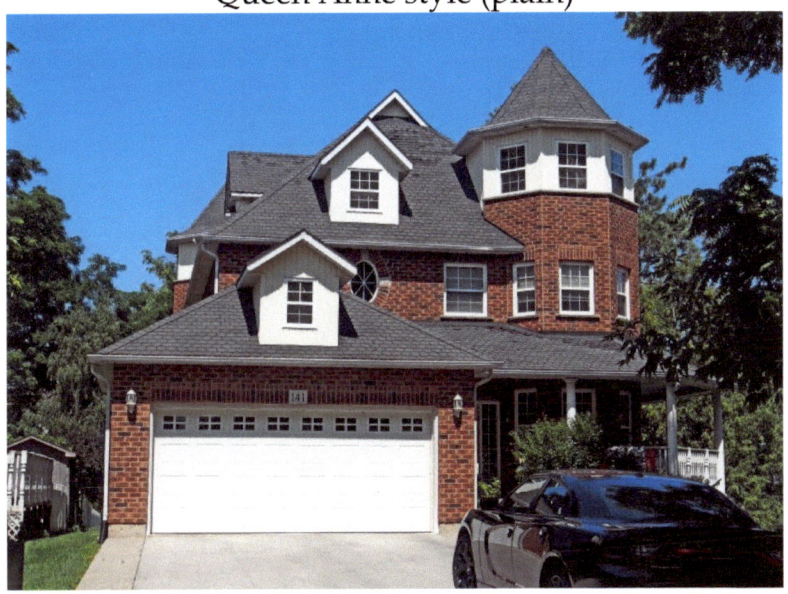

Grimsby Book 2 - 141 Lake Street – storey tower, dormers

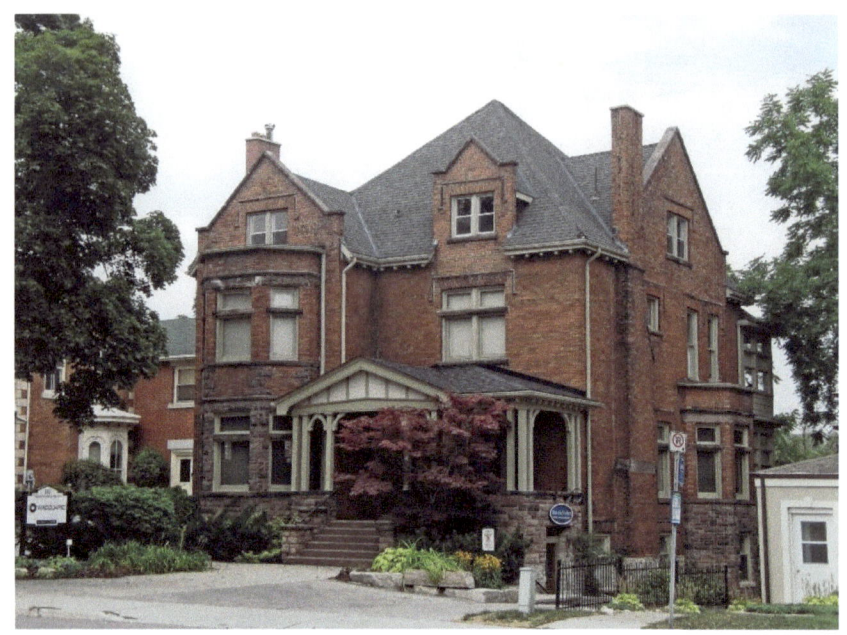

Guelph Book 2 - Red brick – three-storey tower, bay window on side, pediment above verandah

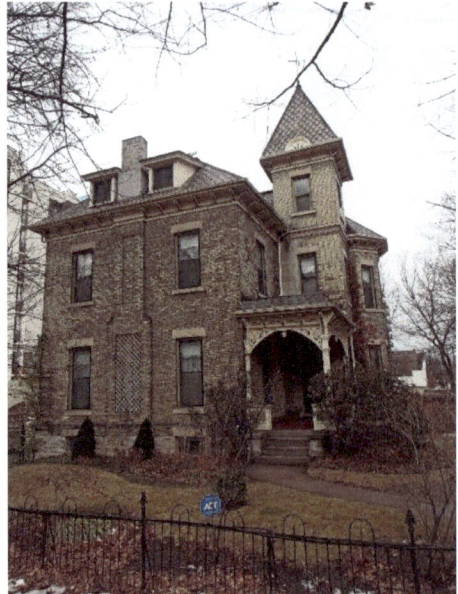

Hamilton Book 1 - 72 Charlton Avenue West – turret, dormers

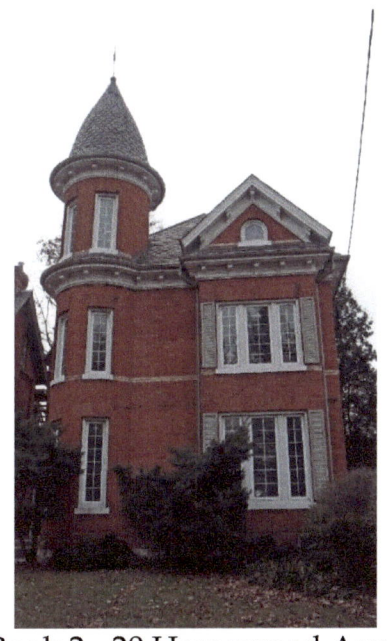

Hamilton Book 2 - 20 Homewood Avenue - turret

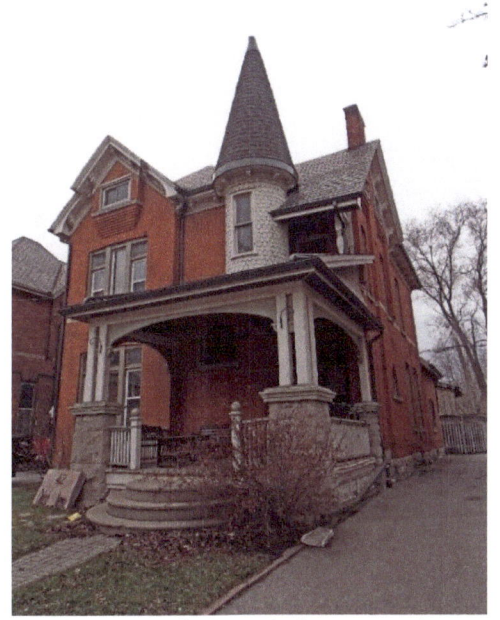

Hamilton Book 3 - 42 Ontario Avenue

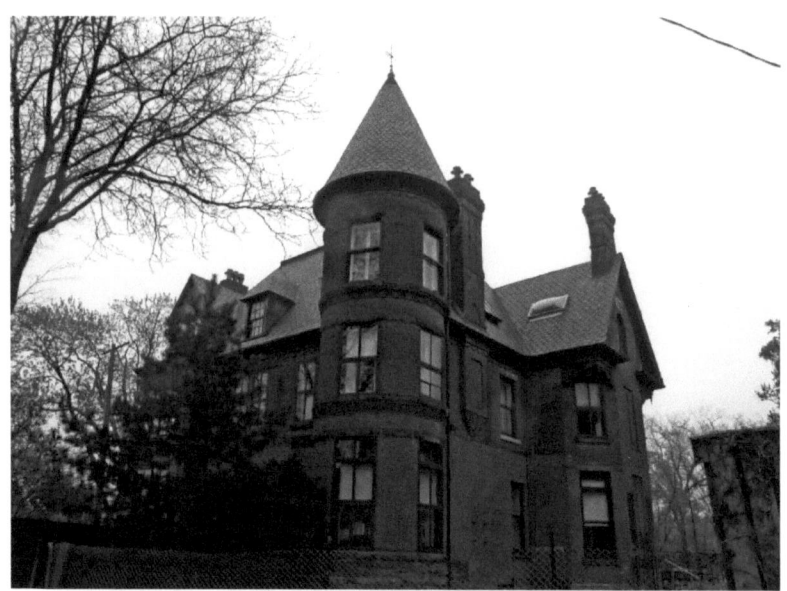

Hamilton Book 4 - 301 Bay Street South (corner of Markland) – built 1890, three-storey turret

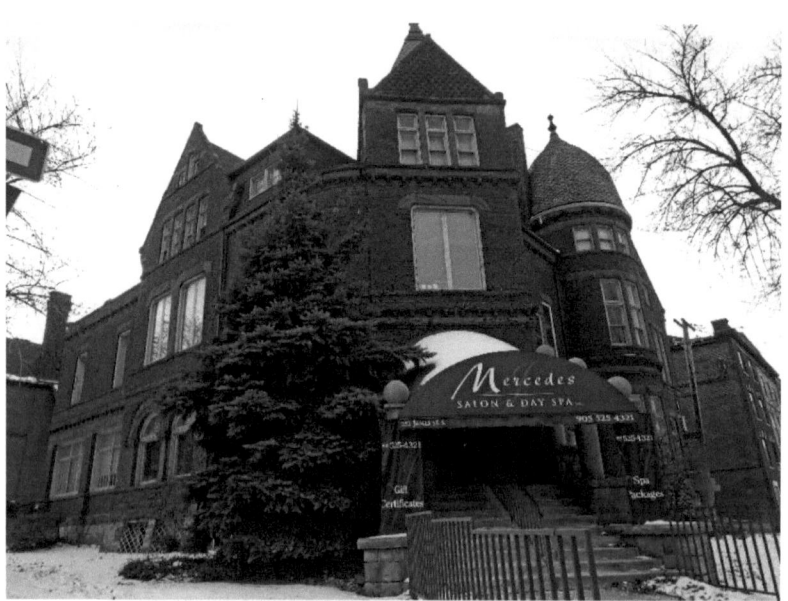

Hamilton Book 5 - 252 James Street South – turret

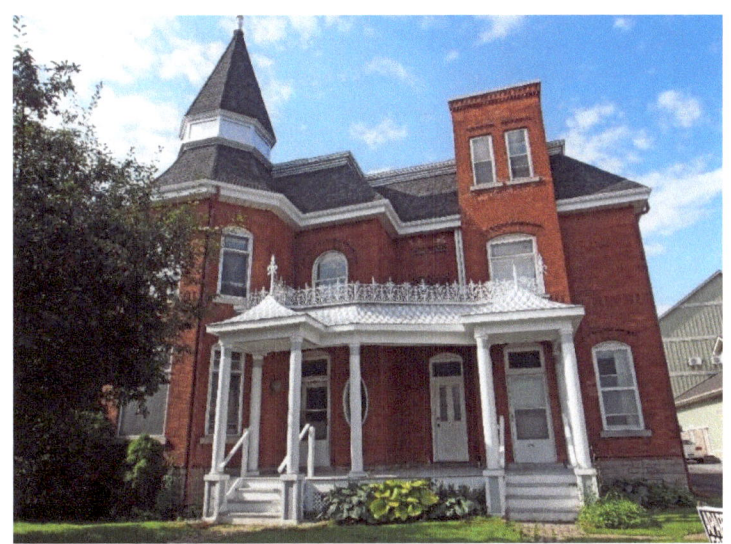

Kemptville - 220-222 Prescott Street – de Pencier House – 1897- brick – tower, turret, iron cresting

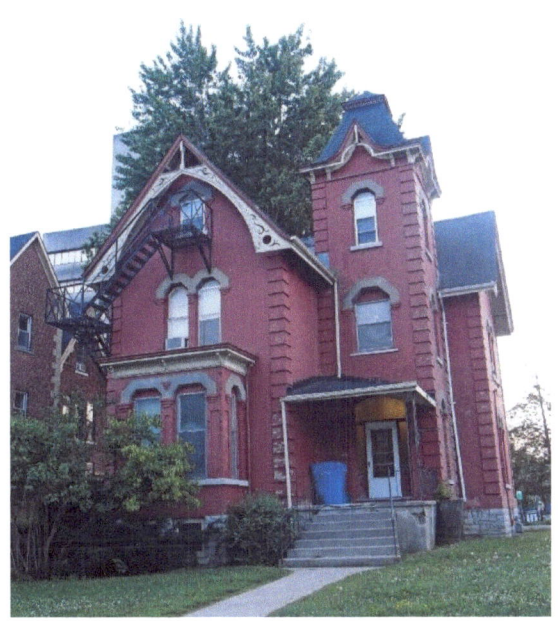

Kingston Book 3 - 78 Barrie Street – three storey tower, cornice brackets, corner quoins, verge board trim on gables

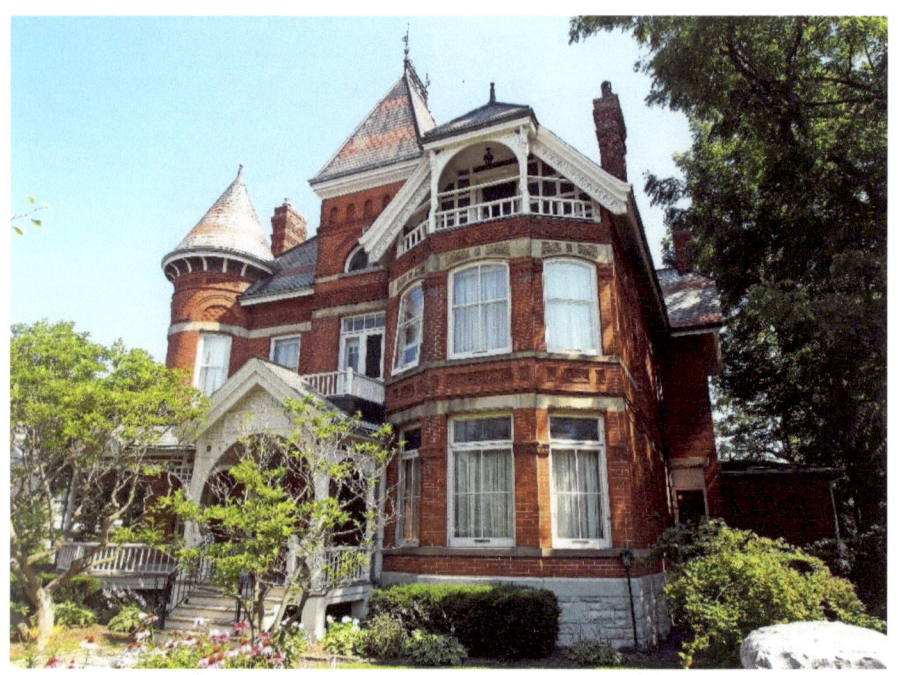

Kingston Book 1 - 95 King Street East – Hendry House – 1886 – high Victorian house in Queen Anne style – asymmetrical design, variety of roof heights and construction materials; terra cotta (hard kiln-fired clay) panels; third floor sleeping porch, turret; dichromatic tile work

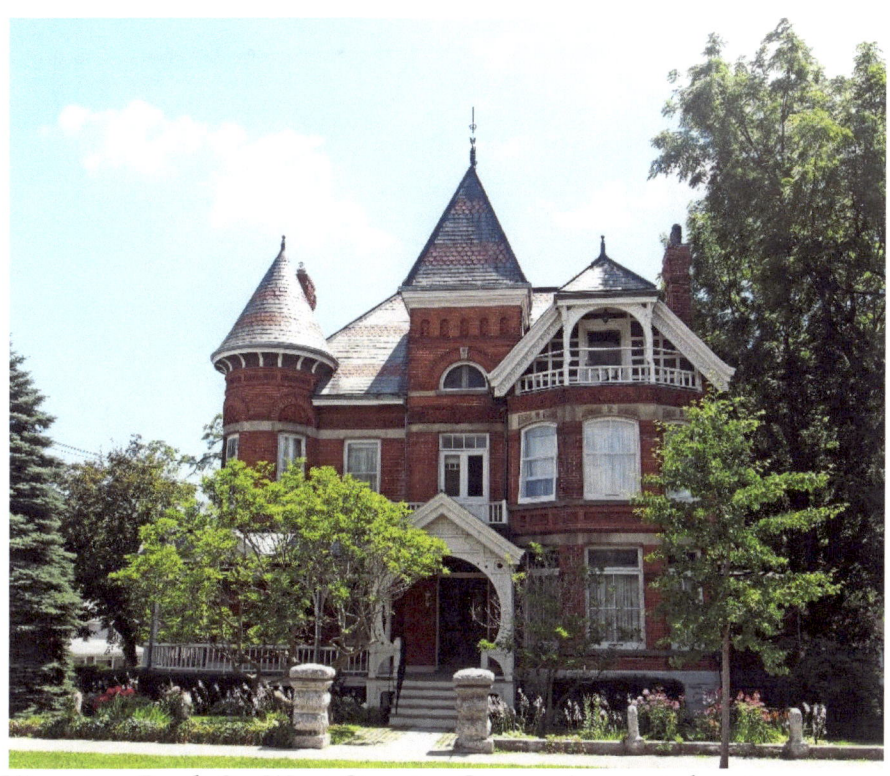

Kingston Book 2 - West Street – Queen Anne style – two-storey turret, 2½ storey central tower, 2½ storey bay window with upper sleeping porch with bargeboard trim on gable; dichromatic tile work; terra cotta decorative brickwork

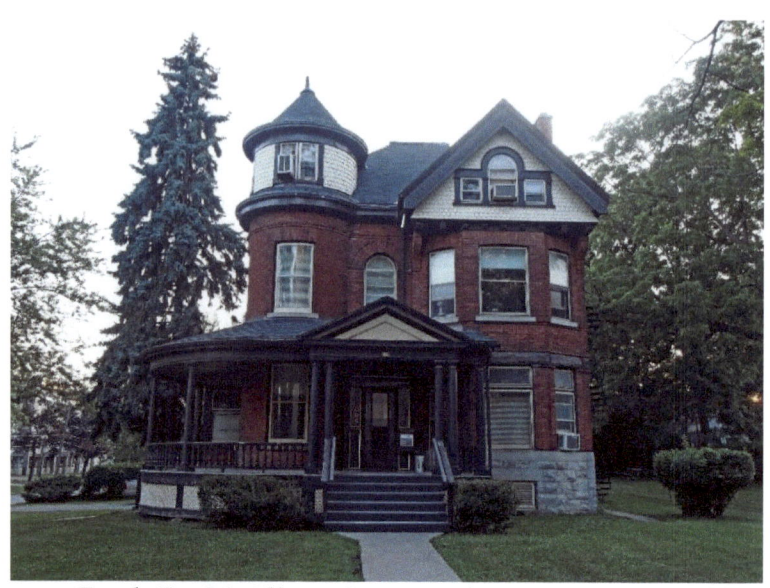

Kingston Book 5 - 96 Albert Street – three-storey turret, Palladian window above two-storey bay window, pediment, voussoirs with keystone

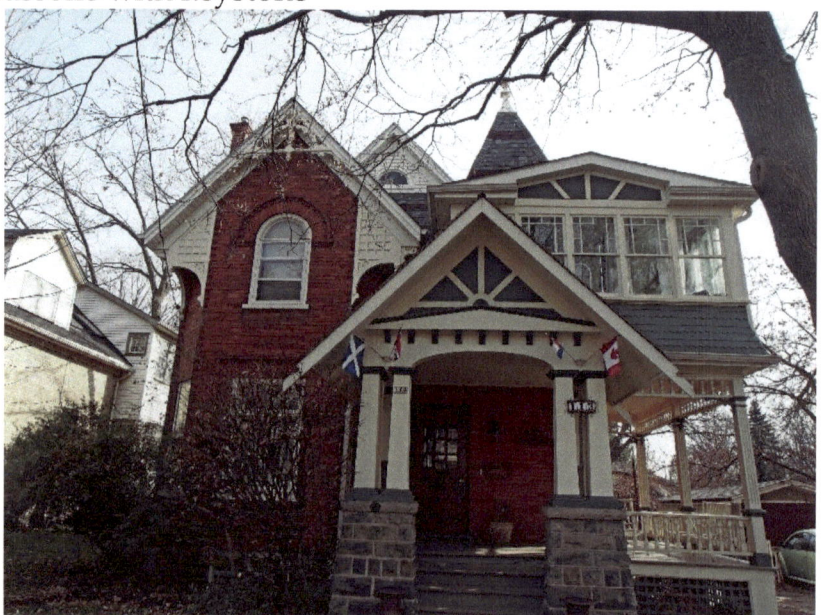

Kitchener Book 1 - 113 Water Street – vergeboard trim, fretwork brackets, second-floor sun room

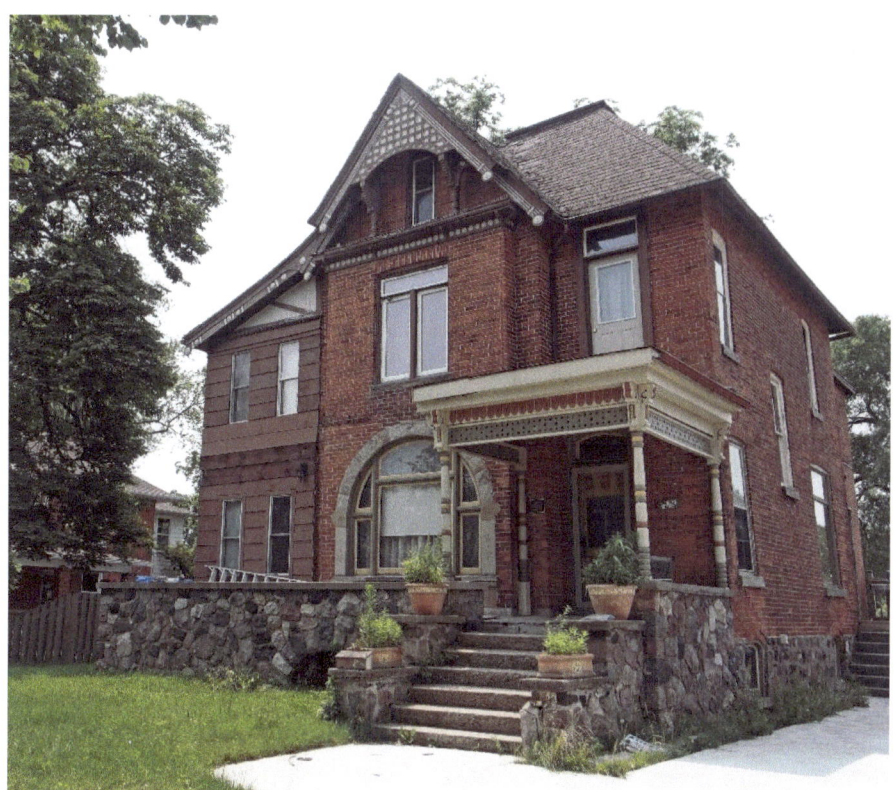

Kingsville Book 1 - 78 Division Street South– built in 1893 - front gable with basket weave cross-bracing with decorative verge boards, fretwork, 2½ story rectangular bay with herringbone brick pattern to separate second storey from attic, cut fieldstone foundation, transom windows, large first storey arched window with rough and smooth stone surround

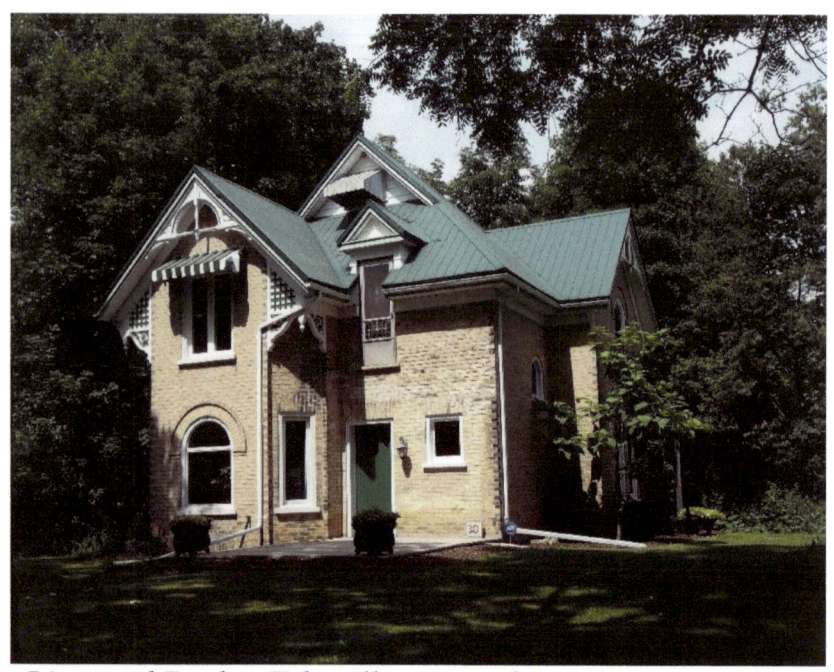

Linwood Book – Erbsville - verge board trim on gables

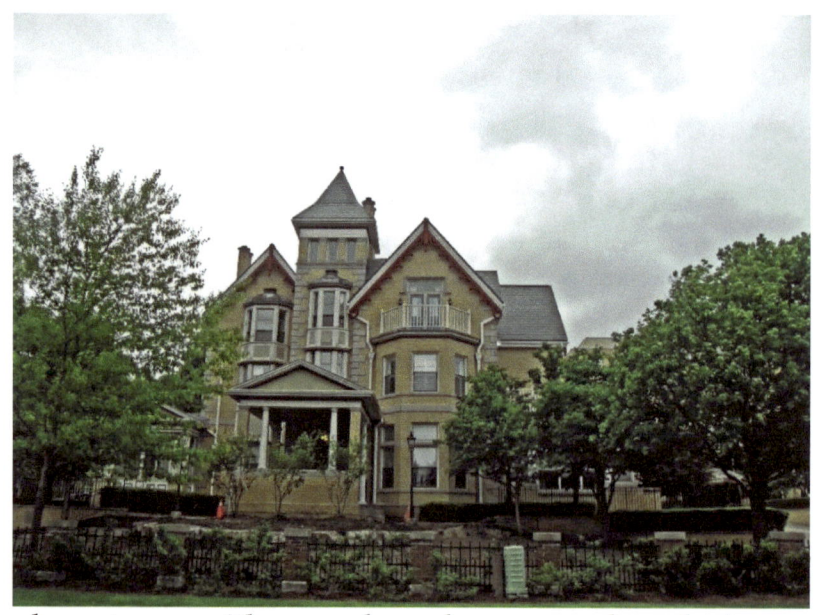

London – tower with cone-shaped cap, vergeboard trim

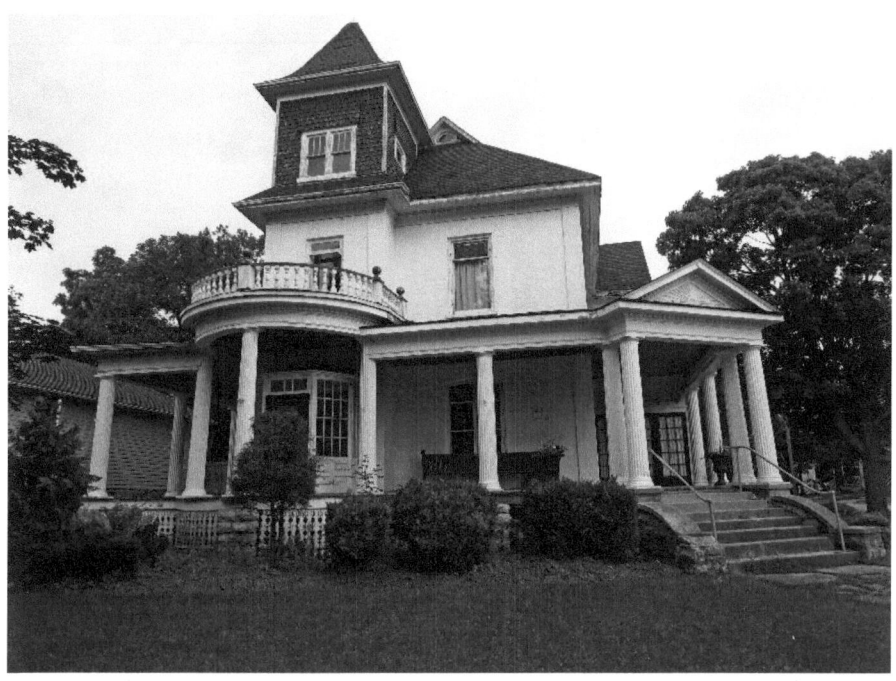

Listowel - 215 Binning Street West – two-storey, white brick, tower, dormer – originally this was a full three storeys high with a Mansard roof; a fire in 1922 damaged the upper level and a new roof was added in the Queen Anne style; spindle railing around circular balcony, Doric pillars, pediment

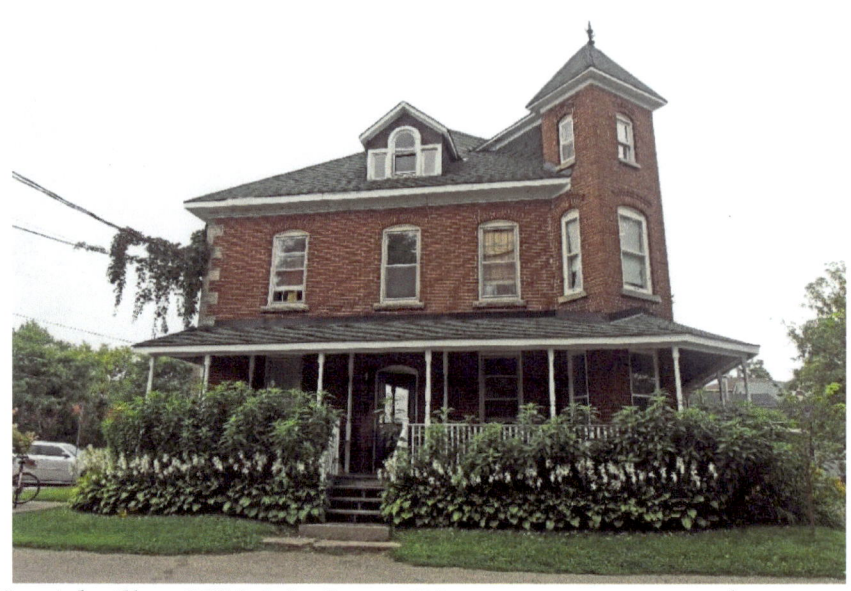

Merrickville - 205 Main Street West – corner tower, dormer with Palladian window, turned veranda roof supports, open railing

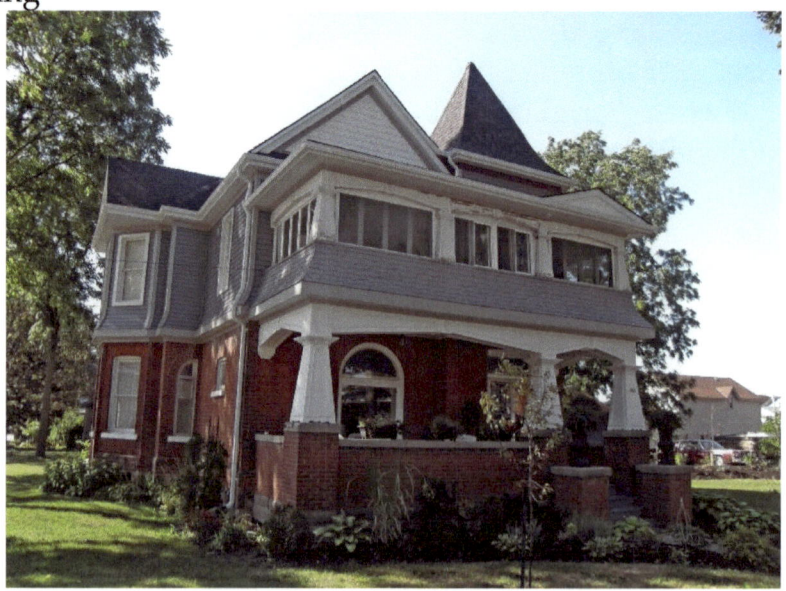

Mitchell - turret

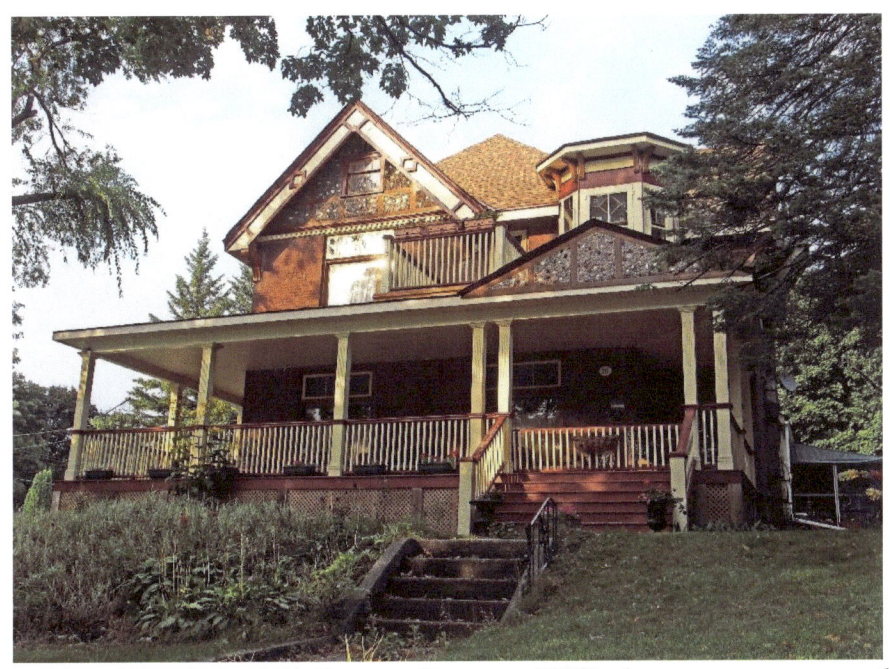

Midland Book 2 - 251 Queen Street – 1875 - large wrap-around veranda, tower, ornate brackets, brick detailing on chimney, multiple roof lines, multi-paned art glass and numerous dormers and gables; decorative solid bargeboard; crushed glass façades beneath the gables; exposed purlins along the roof edges; eyebrow windows, etched glass, stained glass and diamond-shaped decorative paned windows; original stone retaining wall along both Queen Street and Dominion Avenue

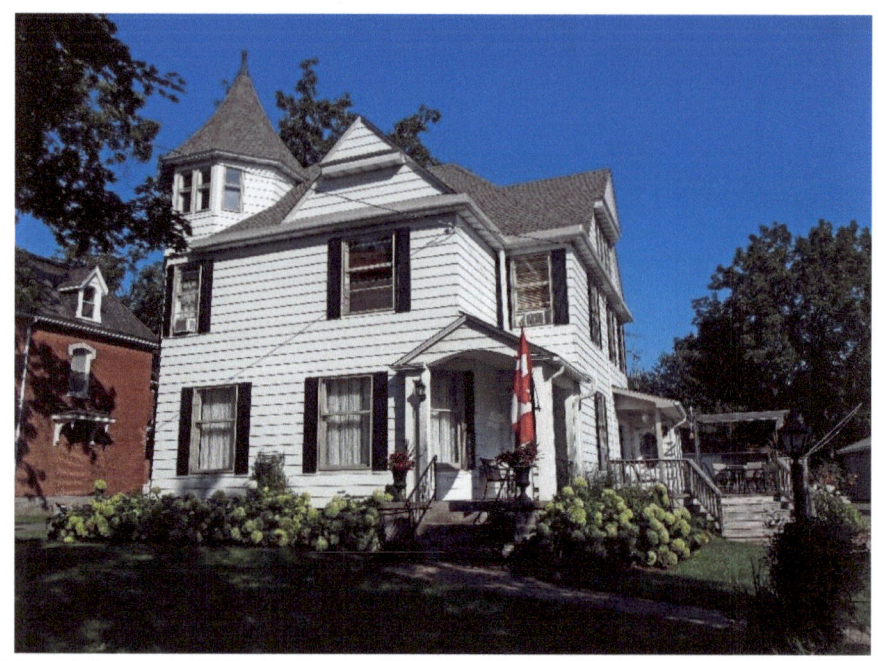

Morrisburg - 12 Lakeshore Drive – irregular massing, steep hip roof, offset tower – original wood cladding has been covered with modern siding

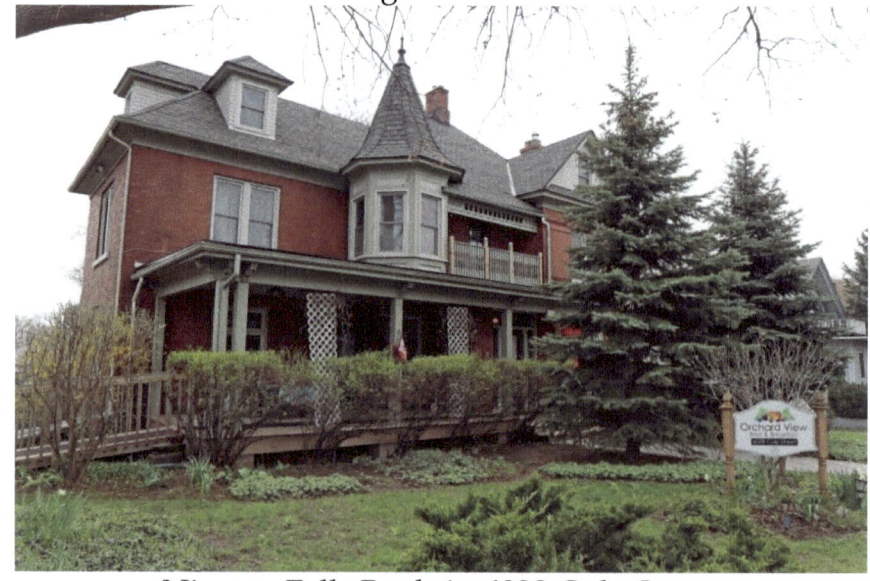

Niagara Falls Book 1 - 6028 Culp Street

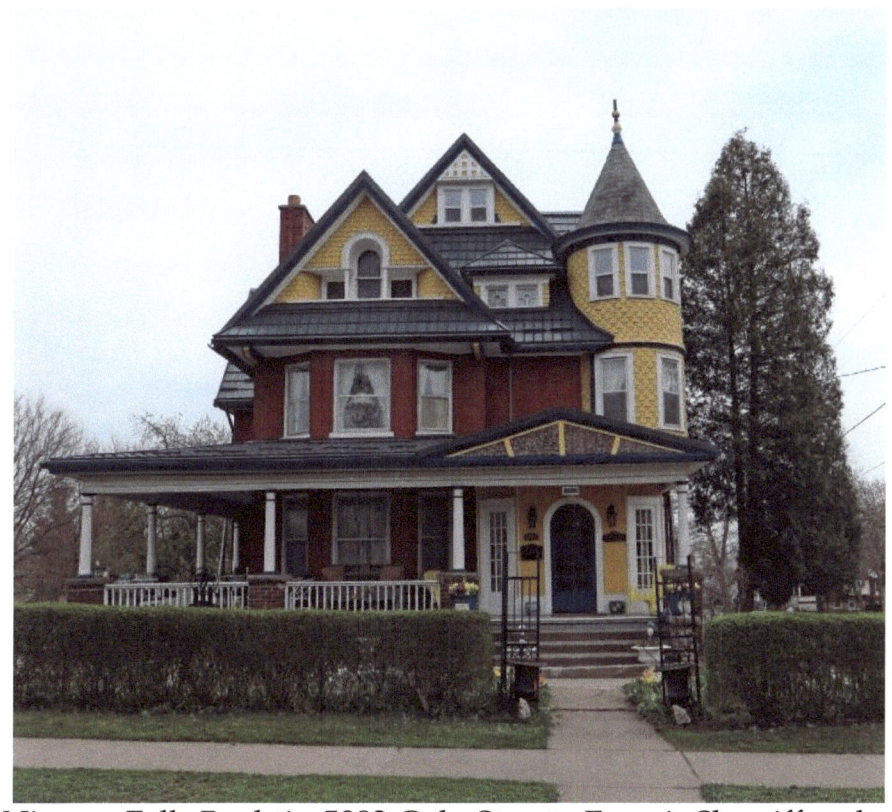

Niagara Falls Book 1 - 5982 Culp Street - Francis Sherriff and Thomas Bright started the *Niagara Falls Wine Company* (Brights Wines) in Toronto in 1874. They moved to Niagara Falls in 1890 to be closer to their major source of grapes. This house was built for Francis Sherriff in 1894 for a cost of $4000.00. It is in the Queen Anne Revival style with an asymmetrical form, deep porch, and an irregular roofline which includes gables, dormers and a turret. The house exterior is brick with decorative cedar shingles on the turret and in the gables. The three-part window in the front gable is an adaptation of the Palladian style; the central section has a round headed window. The large wraparound porch has Tuscan style columns that rest on a brick base topped with a square stone cap.

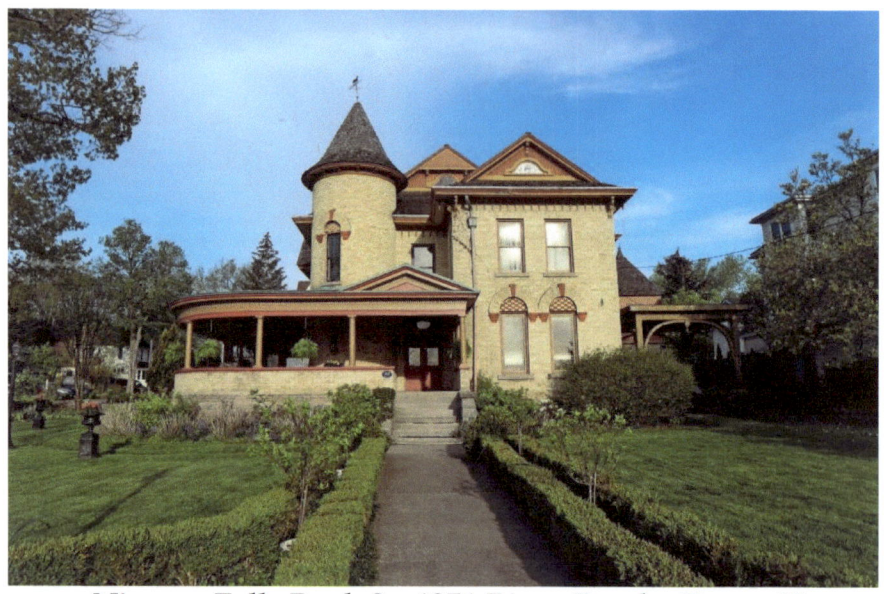

Niagara Falls Book 2 - 4851 River Road – Doran House – 1886 – Park Place Bed and Breakfast - W.L. Doran and his brother owned the Dominion Suspender Company and Niagara Necktie Factories in town. The house served as an unofficial social club and was the scene of both formal balls and many a wild party.

Built of fine cream-colored brick, it has a round corner tower with a conical roof, gable windows of various shapes and a curved verandah with a molded frieze supported by slender columns. To the rear of the house is the original detached coach house.

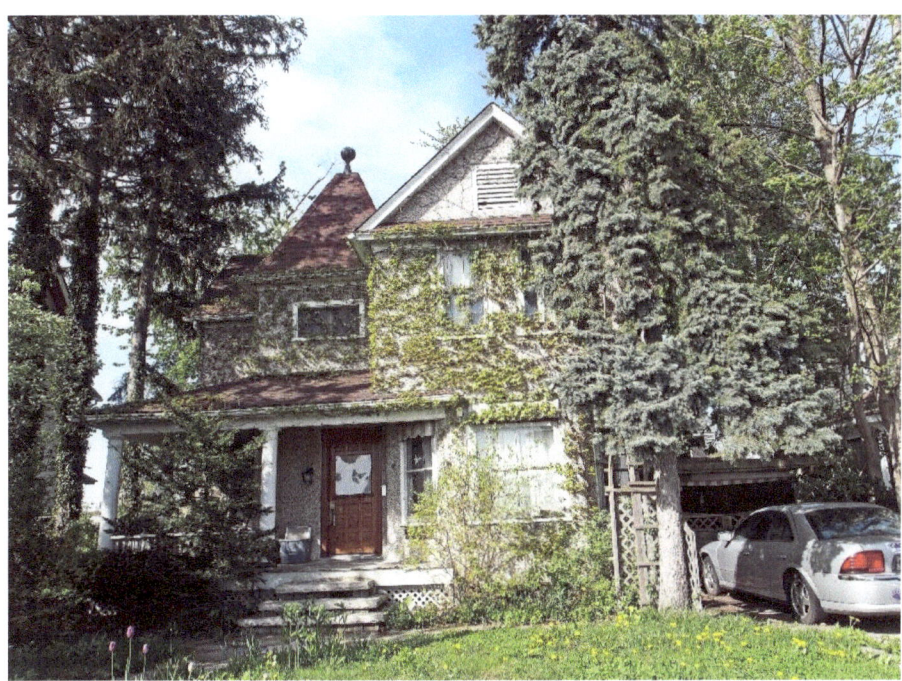

Niagara Falls Book 3 - 4888 Hunter Street – This Queen Anne Revival style house was originally covered in clapboard and later with stucco. The square front tower is topped with a peaked roof and round pommel-like copper finial. Every other floor joist is a half log and the foundation walls appear to be earth and rubble.

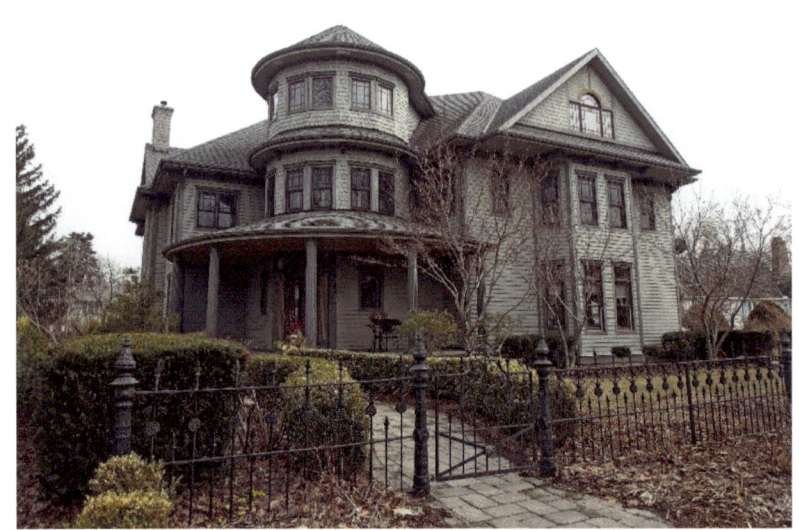
Niagara on Lake Book 1 - 116 Front Street – turret, Palladian window

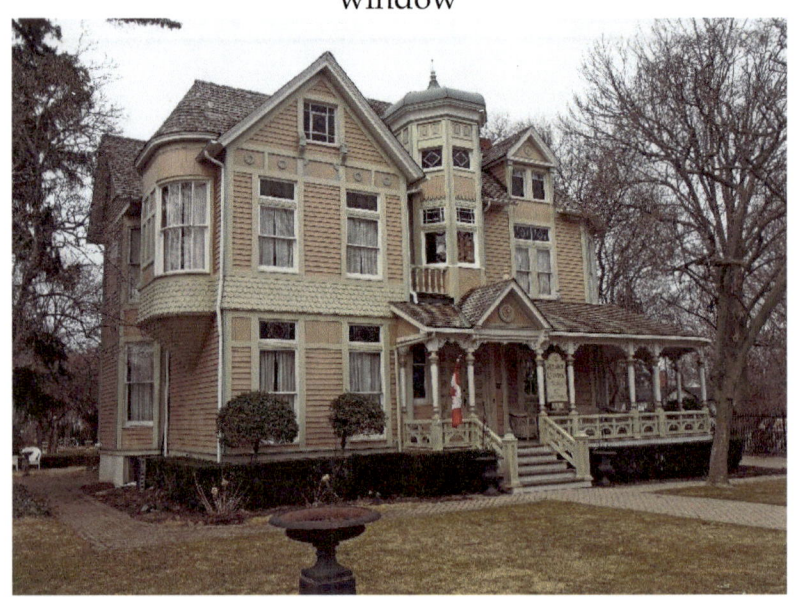
Niagara on Lake Book 2 - 177 King Street – The Romance Collection Gallery featuring the exclusive works of Trisha Romance and Tanya Jean Peterson

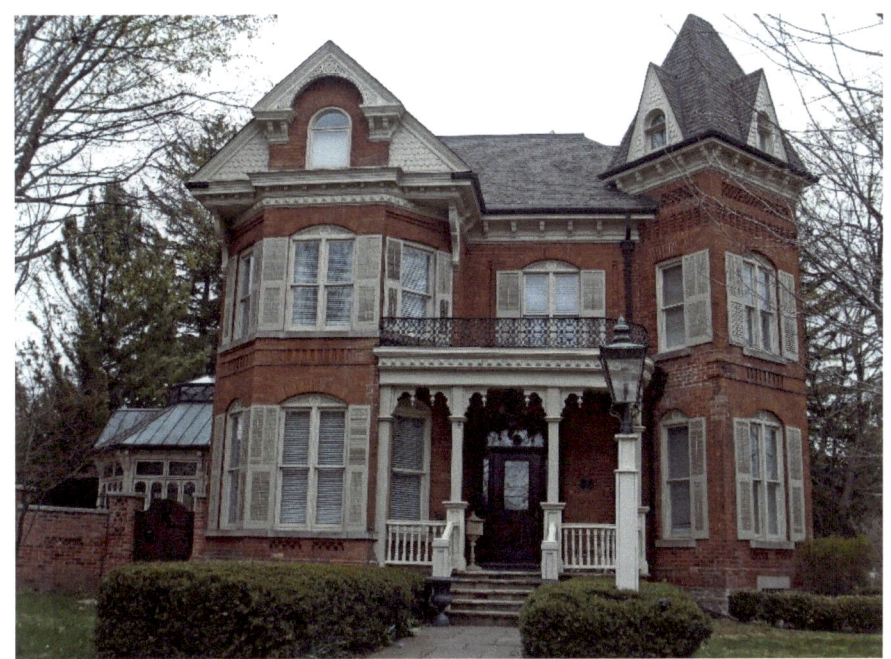

Oakville - 43 Dunn Street – towers, bay windows, balcony on second floor, cornice brackets - Cecil Marlatt's estate

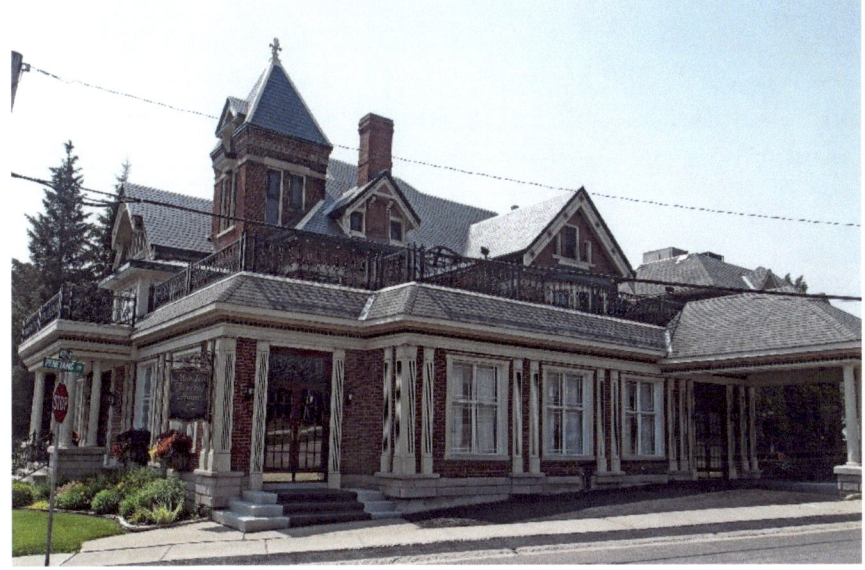

Orillia - 79 West Street North - Mundell Funeral Home - second floor balcony

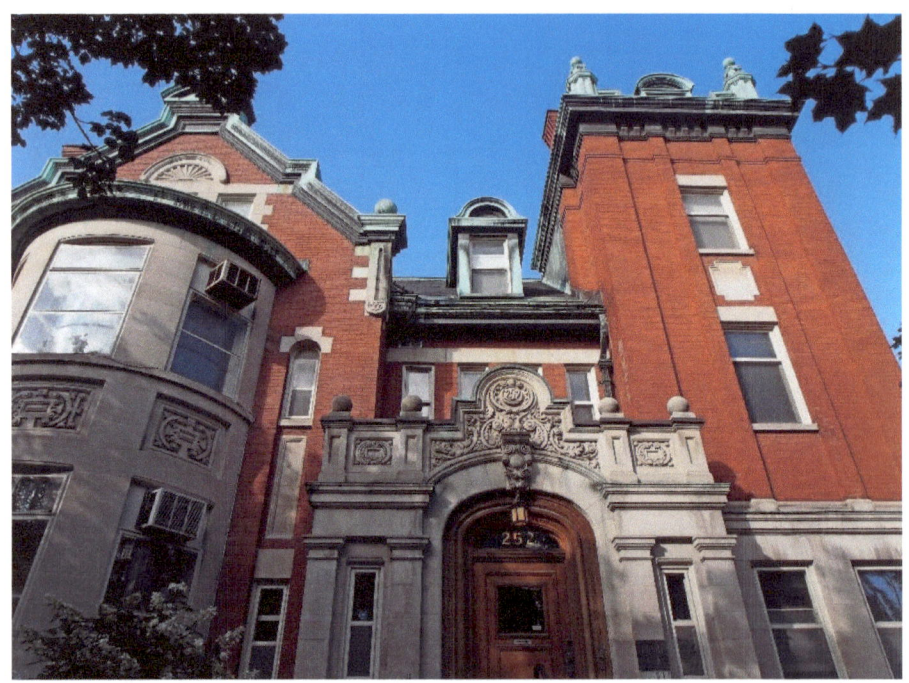

Ottawa Book 2 - 252 Metcalfe Street – Queen Anne Revival – built by lumber baron John R. Booth 1906-1909 – elaborately shaped gables, ornate stone moulding, intersecting ridges of the roof

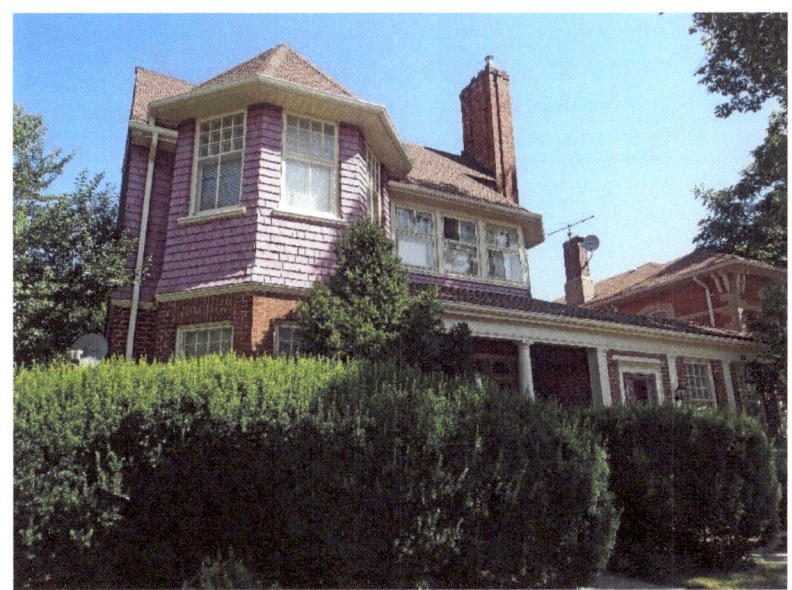

Orangeville Book 2 - 239 Broadway – Aiken House built in 1896 – turret, gambrel roof, chimney with vertical pilaster-like brick work detail

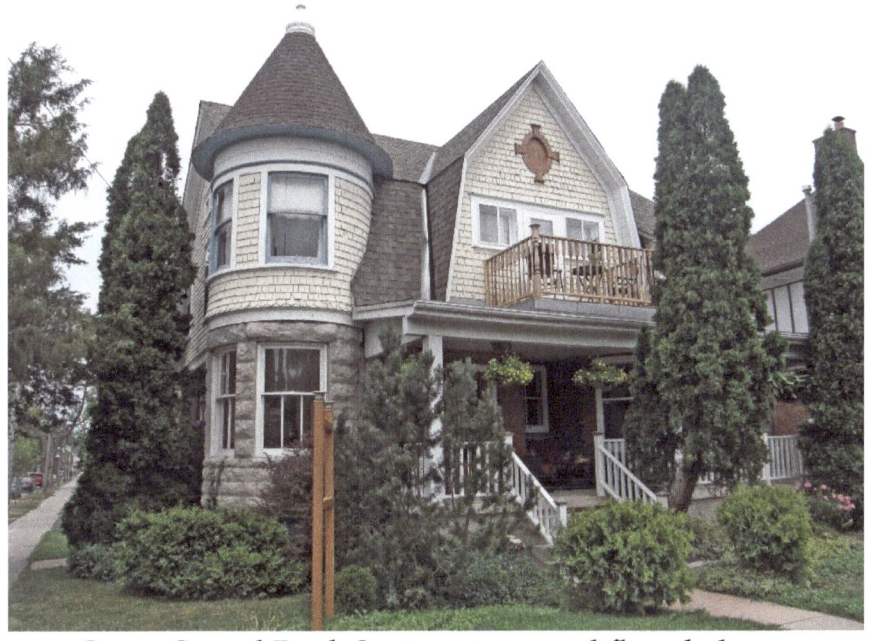

Owen Sound Book 2 – turret, second floor balcony

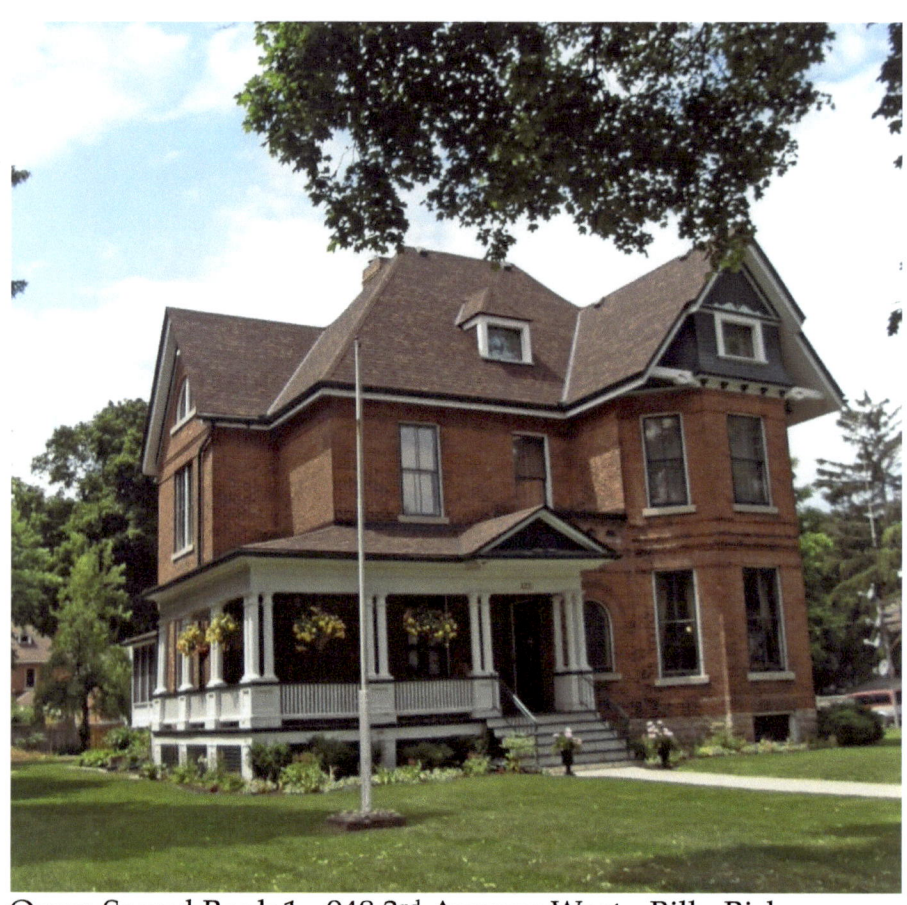

Owen Sound Book 1 - 948 3rd Avenue West - Billy Bishop Home and Museum - Built 1884 – Queen Anne Revival style, asymmetrical proportions, a variety of window shapes and decorative millwork

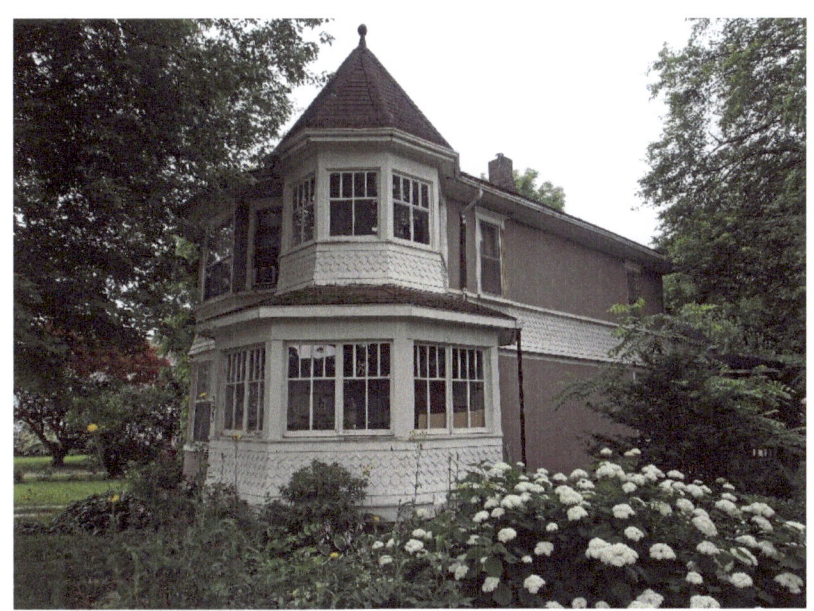

Palmerston - 325 William Street – turret

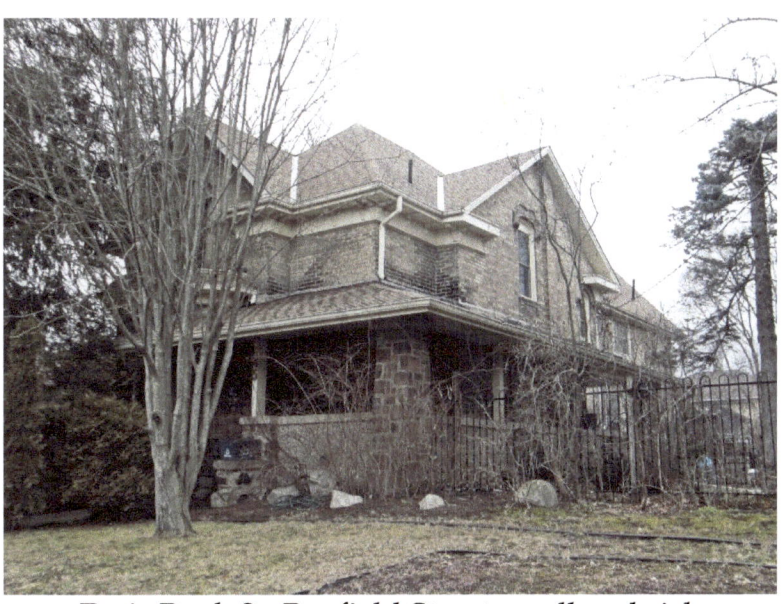

Paris Book 2 - Banfield Street – yellow brick

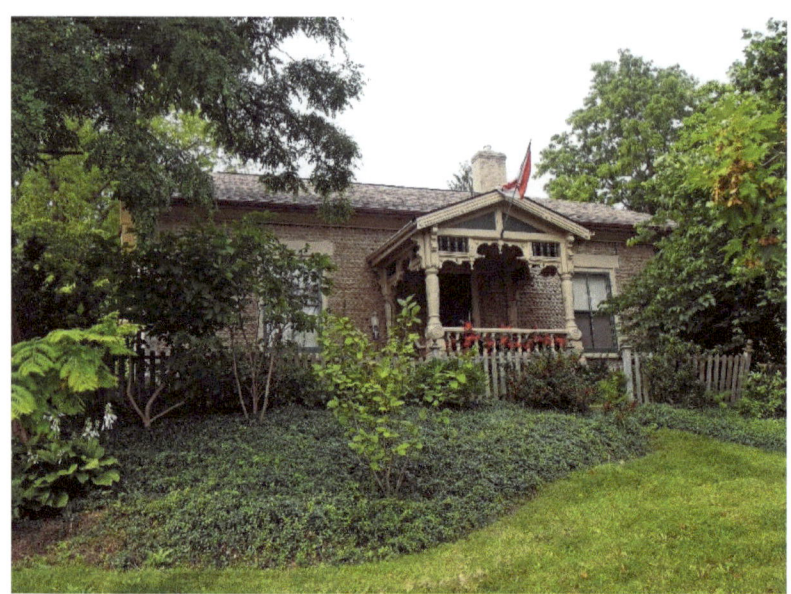

Paris Book 1 - 22 Church Street – Dr. Alfred Bosworth and his wife Sarah built their home in 1845. It is in the Queen Anne Regency style and has cobblestones on the front and south facades and cut fieldstones on the other two sides.

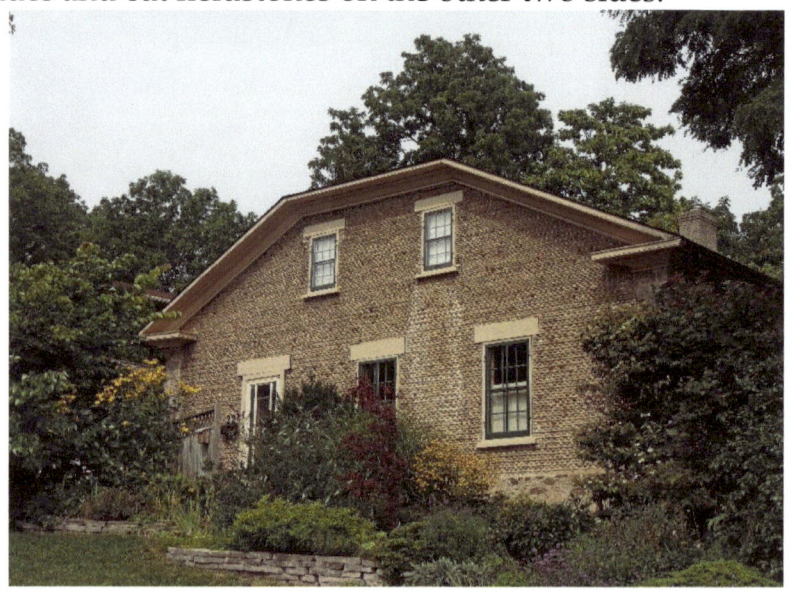

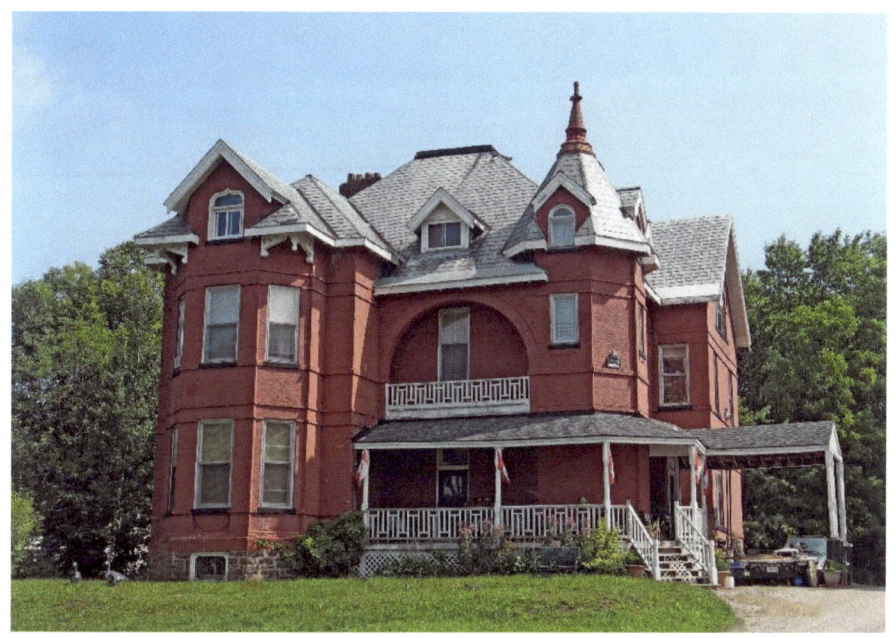

Penetanguishene - 83 Fox Street – 1885 – home of Charles Beck and Amelia Dalms who had nine children (6 boys, 3 girls) – fretwork, turret, dormer, second-floor balcony, string courses wrap around the house; unique shape of window in gable

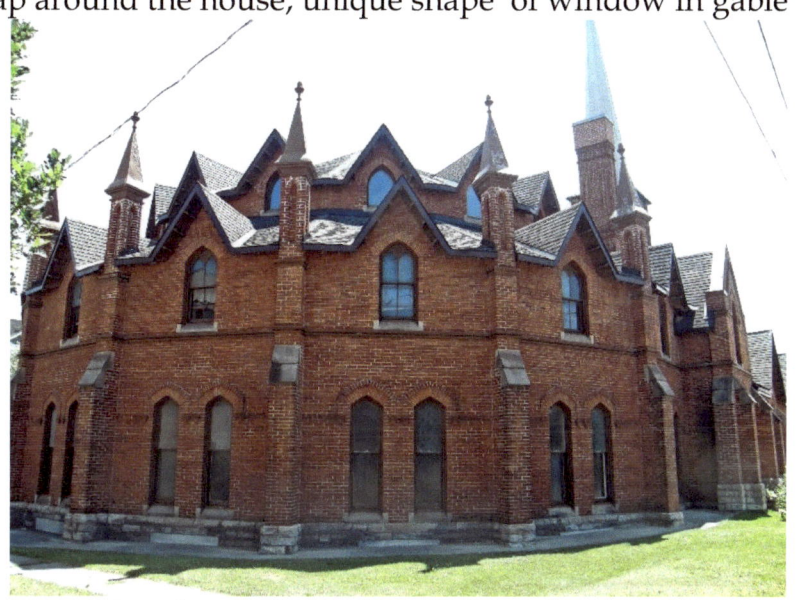

Peterborough Book 3 - Police – buttresses

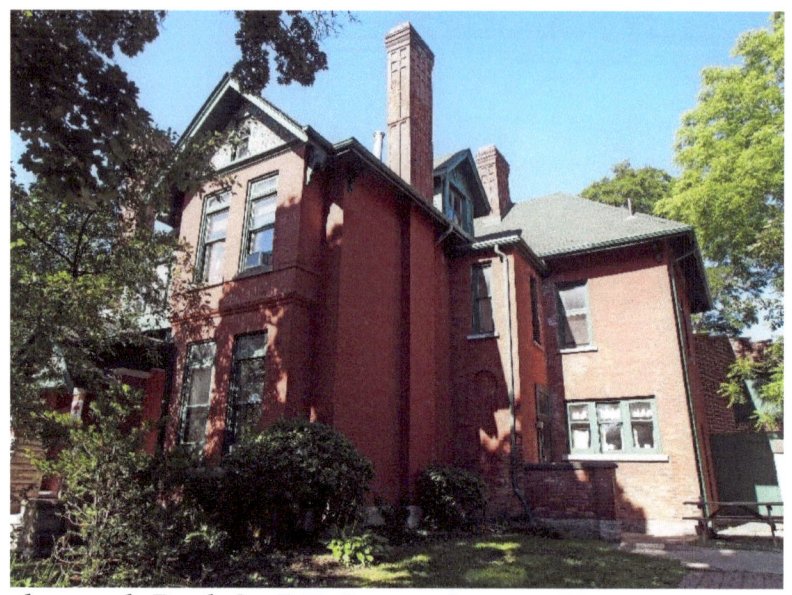

Peterborough Book 2 - 565 George Street – Harstone House 1886 – The Harstone family lived here from 1907 to 1982, when the Red Cross bought the house.

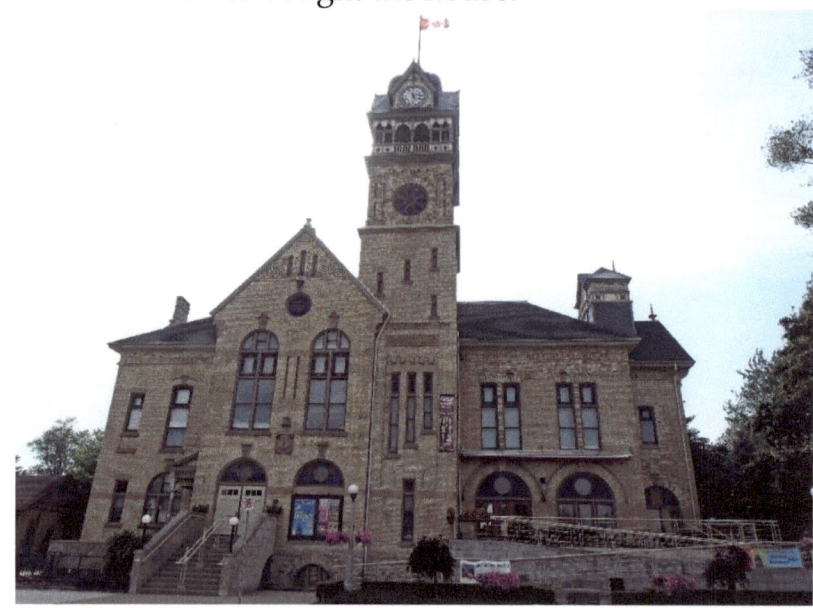

Petrolia - 411 Greenfield Street – Town of Petrolia Municipal Offices - rose windows

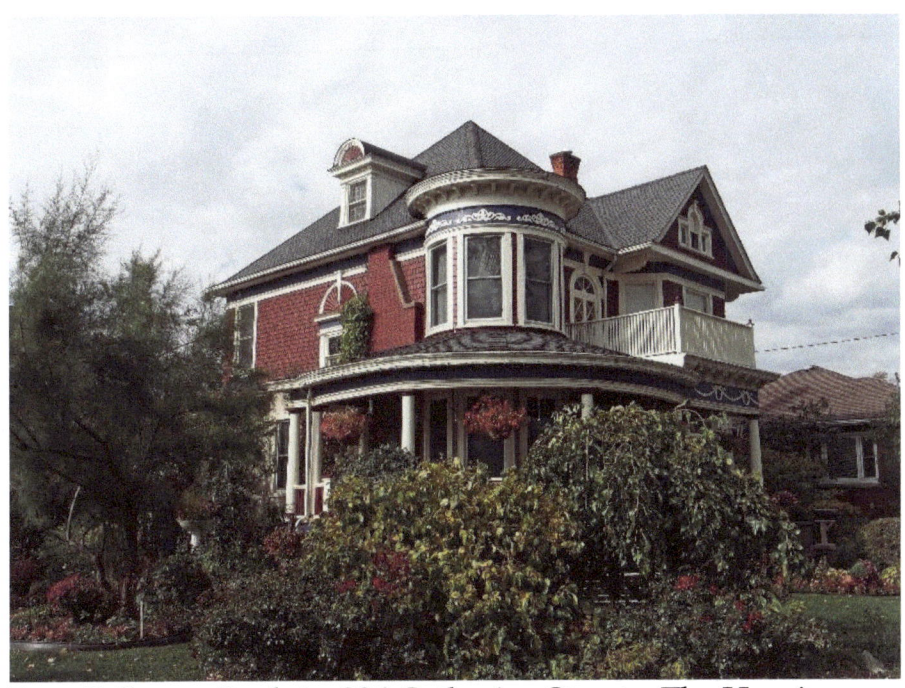

Port Colborne Book 1 - 326 Catharine Street – The Harvie House built in 1900, it is a typical Queen Anne Revival style home and has a wraparound verandah with offset circular tower, two types of siding and a pyramidal roof. The house takes its name from the Harvie family who owned it from 1911 to 1951.

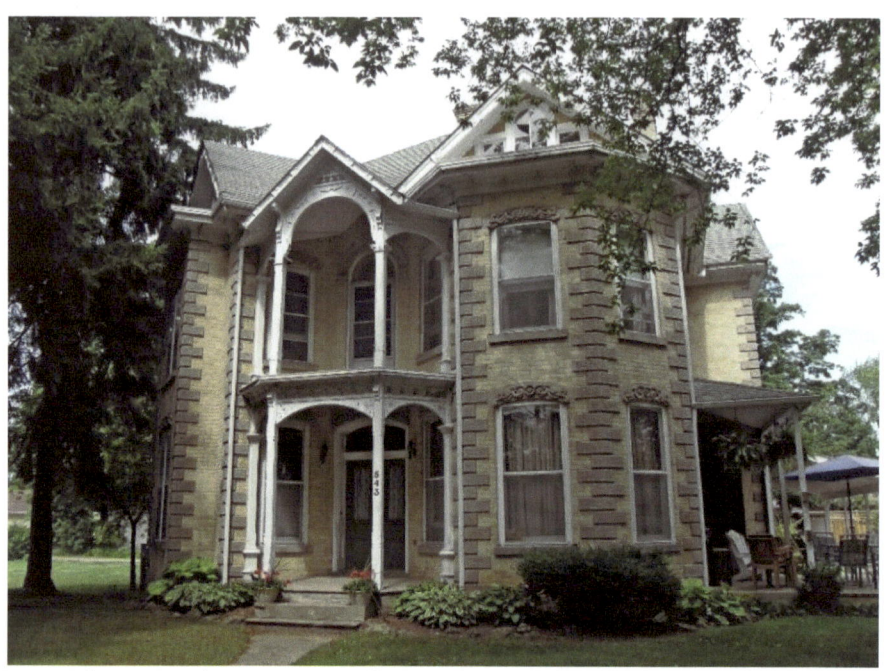

Port Elgin Book 1 - 543 Mill Street – yellow brick, quoins, Palladian windows in gables, large fretwork pieces resembling brackets on eaves of second floor porch, decorative window hoods

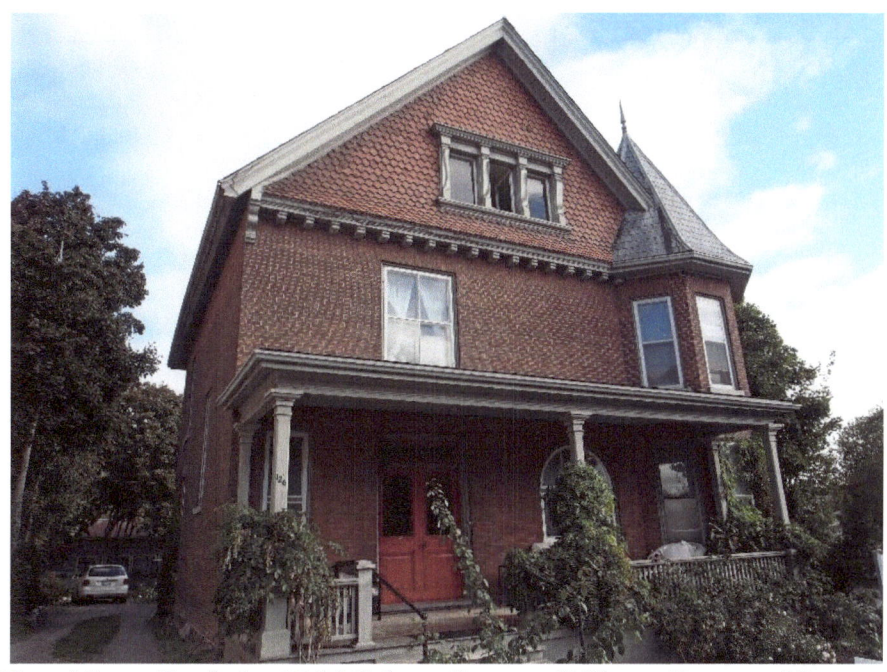

Port Hope Book 1 - 126 Walton Street - Wilson-Benson House – c. 1885 - This two and a half storey brick house is built in the Queen Anne Revival style with an offset tower, a broad verandah, and a steeply pitched roof. The gable on the Walton Street facade is sheathed in decorative shingle. The tower is five-sided with a conical roof topped by a finial and contains a long window on each storey of each wall surface. The large main floor window is Edwardian in treatment with coloured glass in the semi-circular transom section. For fifty years, the Wilsons were publishers of the Port Hope Guide.

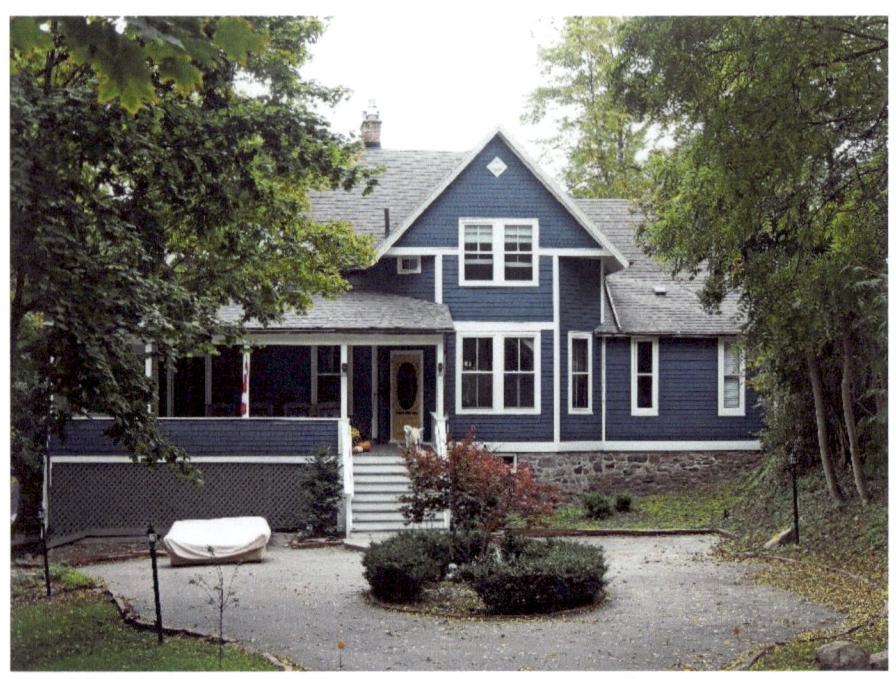

Port Hope Book 2 - 105 Dorset Street West - Bredon House – c. 1880 - This Queen Anne Revival house is often called the Shingle Style. The house is a high storey and a half frame building facing north to Dorset Street and, because of the steep hillside property, on the south side is set over a full storey basement built of squared fieldstone. The highly ornamental and picturesque Dorset Street front is marked by a wide bay dominated by a gable overhanging the splayed sides and another smaller gable adjacent, both with paired windows. A verandah wraps around the end of the house, to become an open deck across the south face. The house was modified in 1900, 1970 and 1986.

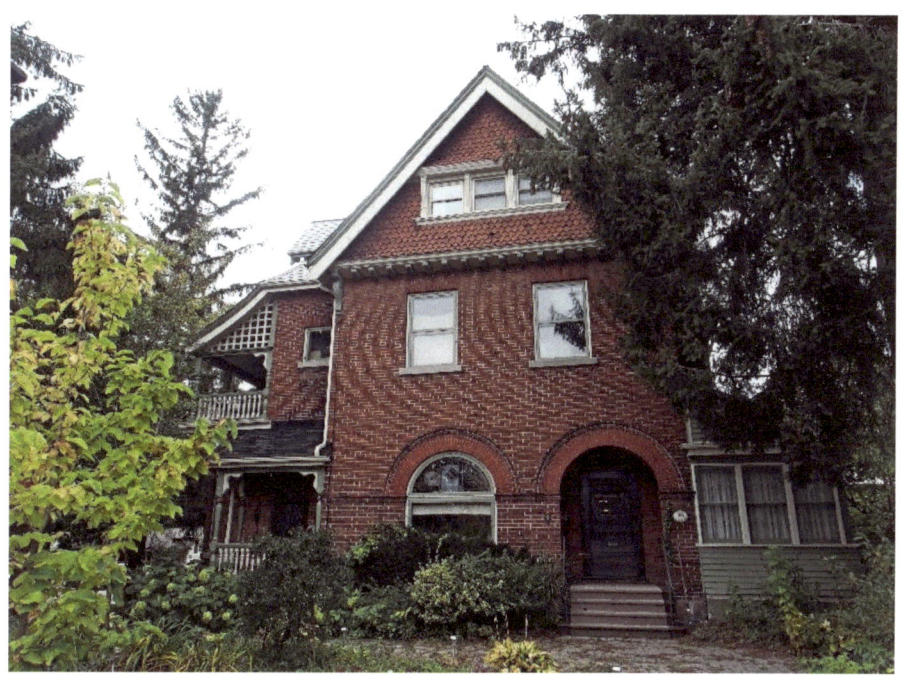

Port Hope Book 3 - 98 Ontario Street - Thomas Wickett House (Penstowe) – c. 1894 - Although built in the Queen Anne Revival style, it has detailing of the Romanesque style. The roof is irregular and complicated, but is composed basically of several steeply pitched gables and one overhanging gable dormer. The gables are pedimented with some rafters exposed. The pediment has a set of triple windows in a bold wooden surround. Trimming the windows are tooled pilasters and heavy entablature. Decorative shingles complete the pediment.

     The stretcher-bond brick house has various types of structural openings from flat on the top storey, to segmental on the projecting south bay, to rounded Romanesque on the front facade. Voussoirs head most windows, but protruding arched gables of brick surround the semi-elliptical openings. Stringer courses join the sills of the house and join the tips of the arches on the main facade. The main door is set in one of the arched openings, but is itself flat.

Another striking feature of the house is a second-storey bell-cast balcony adorned with heavy turned balusters and turned columns. The balcony roof is supported by brackets and has a molded frieze. The open end of the balcony is partially filled by lattice-like woodwork. The spooled columns are turned and have a rounded, bulbous appearance. On the first storey, a shed-roofed porch with the same characteristics can be seen. The house sits on a squared-stone foundation with segmental basement windows.

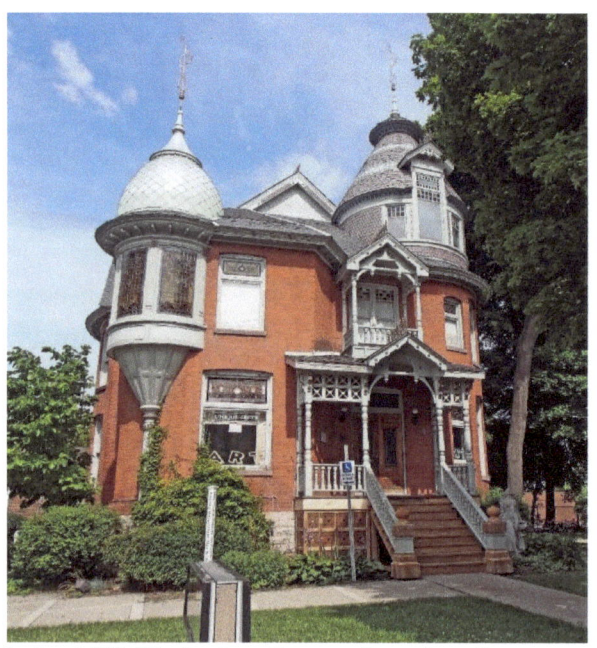

Sarnia Book 1 - 127 Christina Street South – Lawrence Family mansion – Mr. Lawrence was a lumberman – 1892

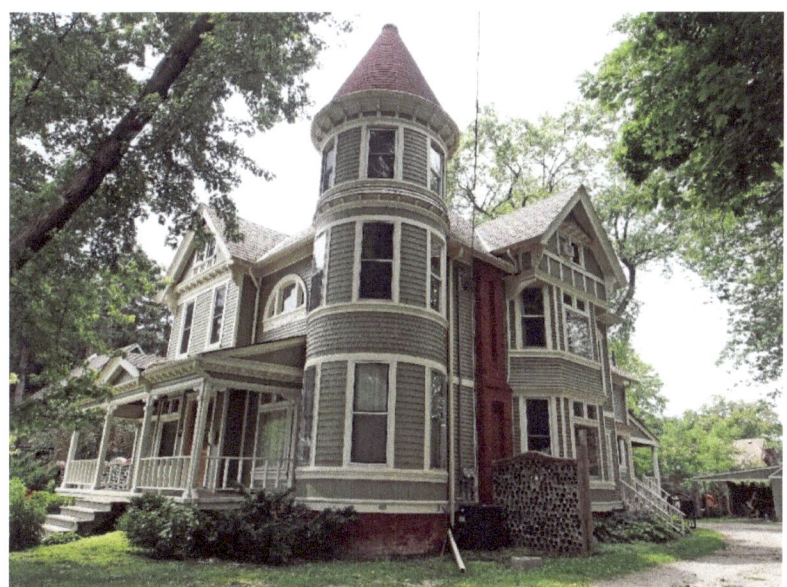

Sarnia Book 4 - 183 Vidal Street South – Queen Anne – three-storey turret with cone shaped roof

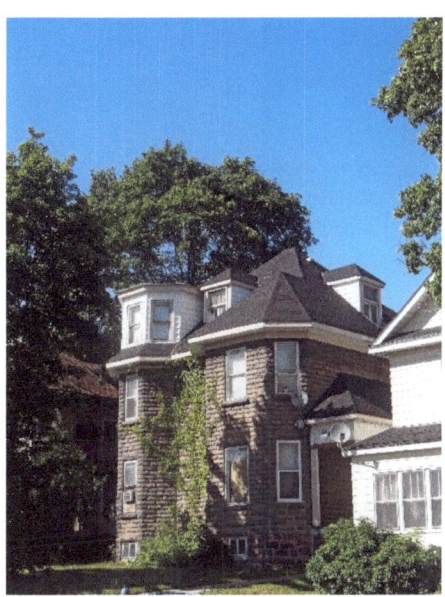

Sault Ste. Marie - 650 Queen Street East – three-storey tower-like bay, dormers

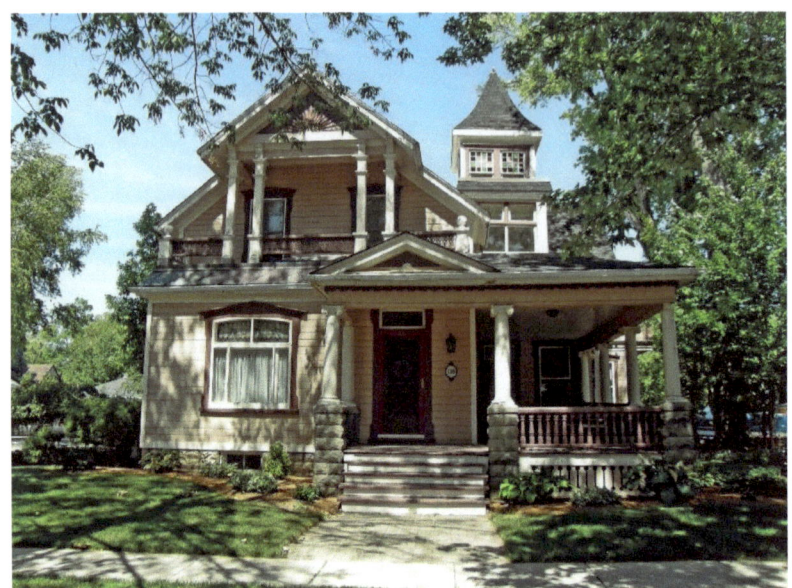

Seaforth - 116 Goderich Street West – belvedere, side verandah

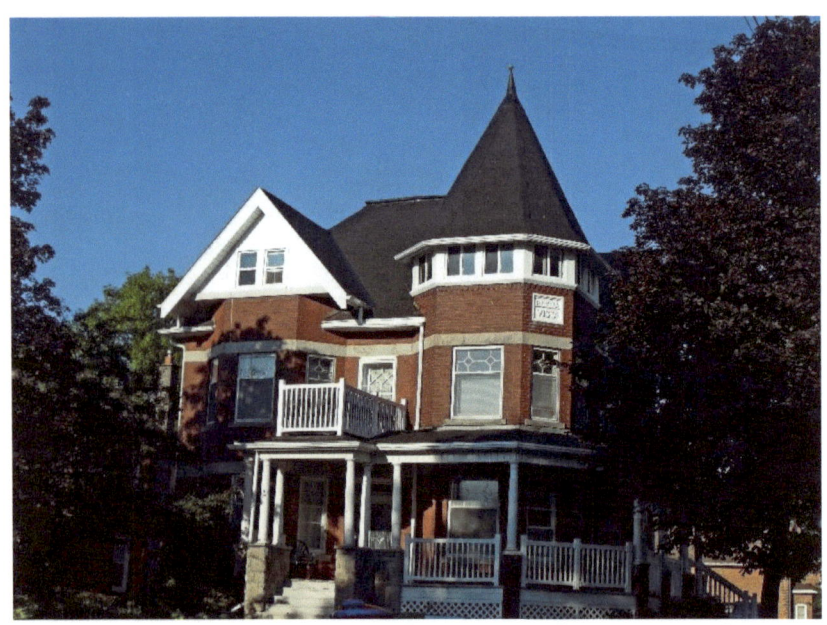

Shelburne - 230 Owen Sound Street at the corner of Second Avenue West - Buena Vista

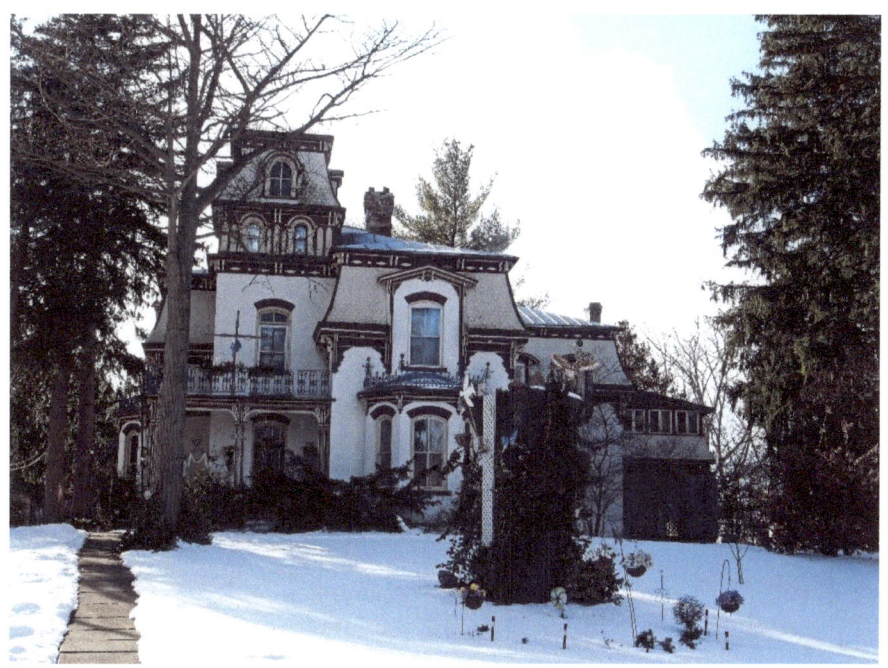

Simcoe - 364 Colborne Street – old castle – four-story tower with iron cresting on top; iron cresting above ground floor bay window, elaborate cornice brackets

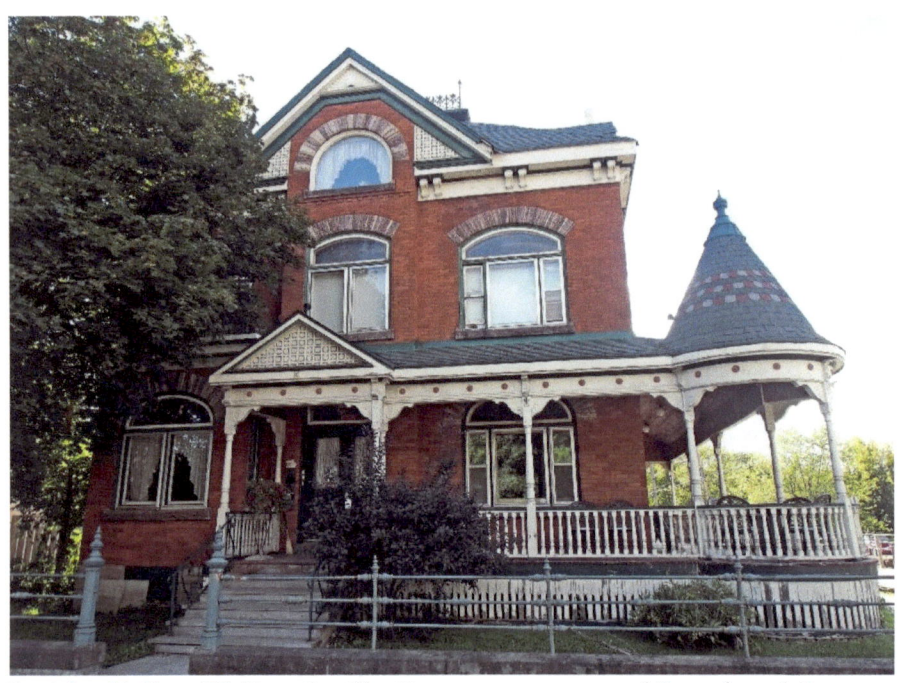

Smiths Falls - 78 Brockville Street at corner of Lombard Street – built by Ogle Carss, an early mayor of the town – 1895 – irregular outline, broad gables, multi-sloped roofs, a belvedere, a tower, ornamental cast iron railings on the roof; long, graceful wraparound verandah; stone voussoirs over semi-circular windows with transoms

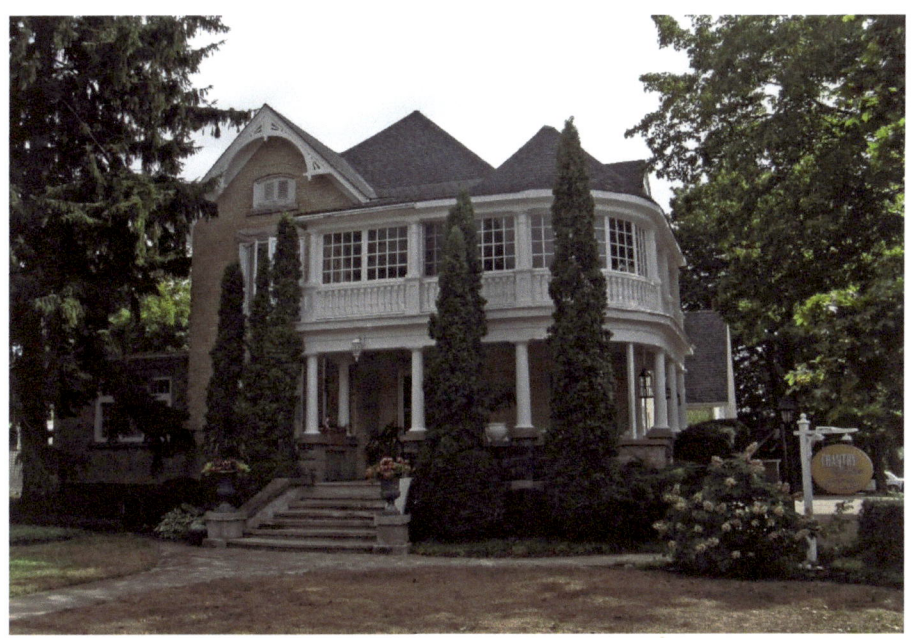

Southampton - 107 High Street - Chantry Breezes Bed and Breakfast - George E. Smith, Customs Officer c. 1907

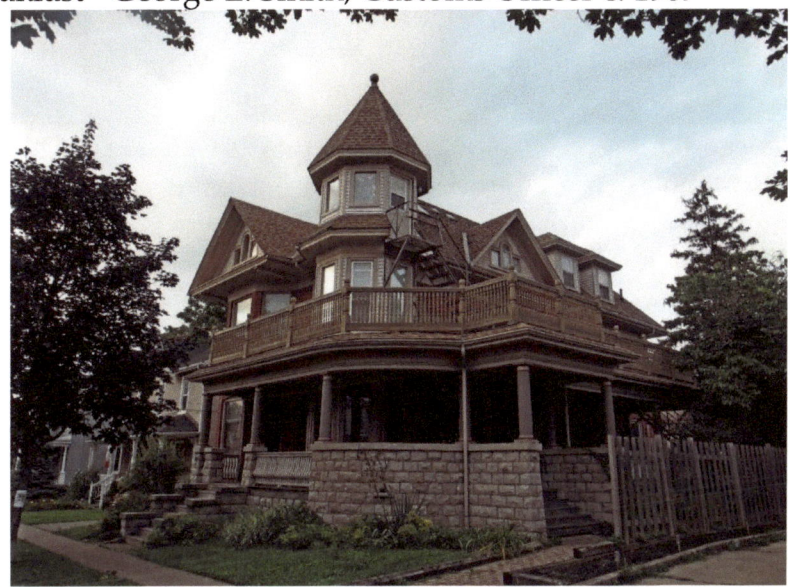

St. Catharines Book 4 - 1 Montebello Place – varied roofline, turret, wraparound veranda on two levels, Palladian windows in gables, dormers

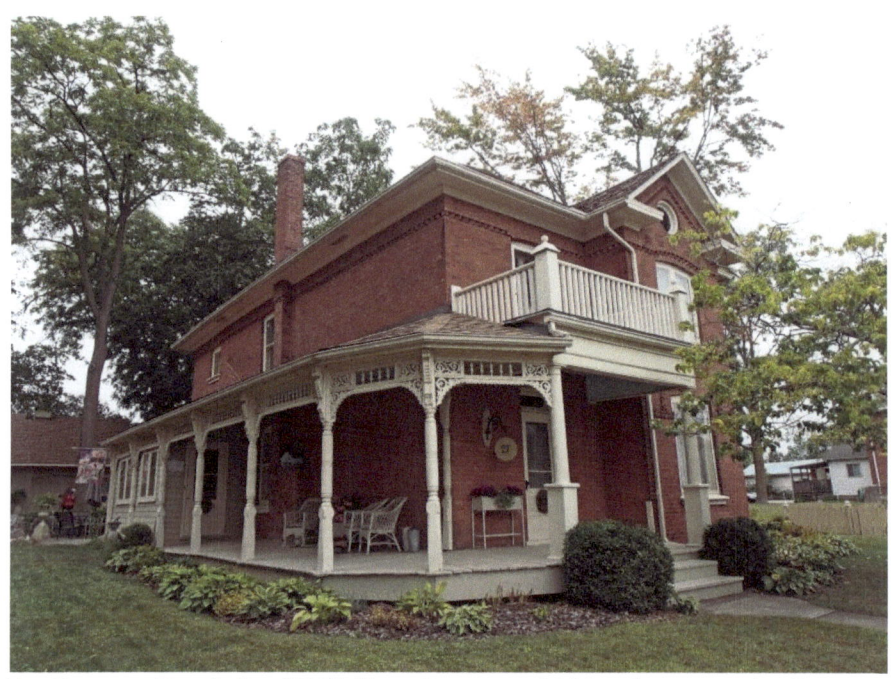

St. George Book 2 - 27 Talbot Street – 1890 – is an early Queen Anne style featuring a wraparound veranda with elaborate scrollwork, spool work and patterned brick work with a stringcourse at the frieze. Rusticated brick is used to ornament the principal window drip mold. Cornice return around the dormer bulls-eye window.

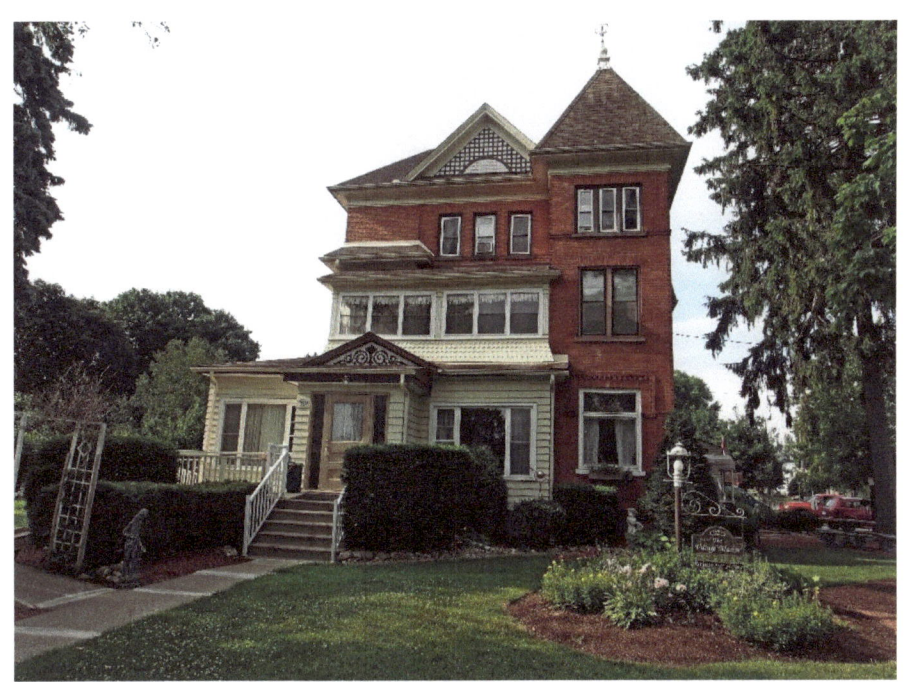

St Jacobs - 29 Albert Street

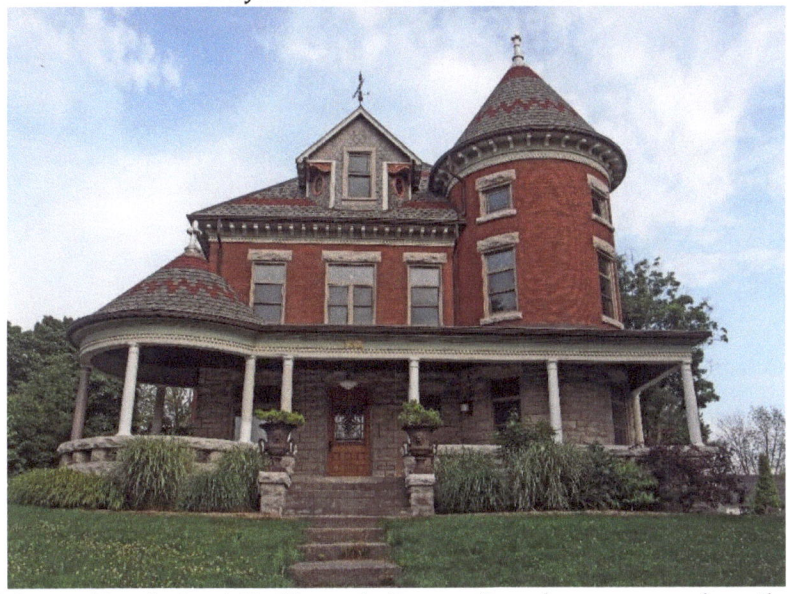

St. Marys Book 1 - 163 Church Street South – turret, dentil moulding, dichromatic tile work, wraparound verandah

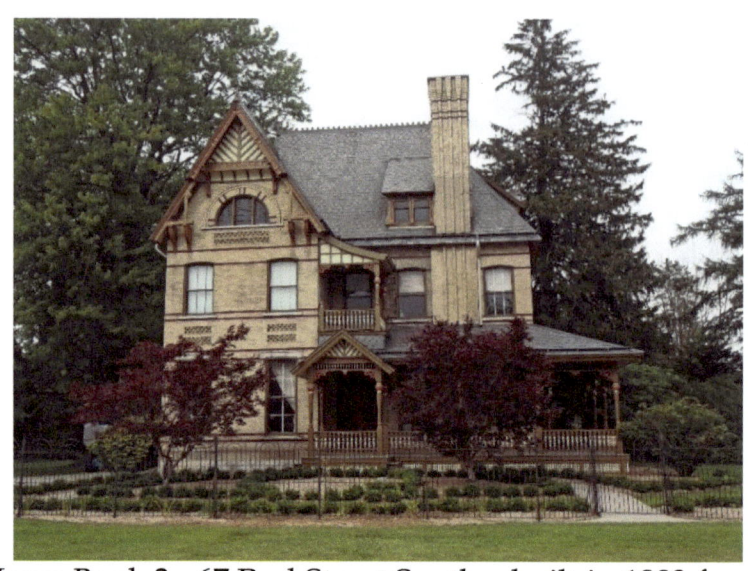

St. Marys Book 2 - 67 Peel Street South – built in 1883 for James Carter (wife Mary Box), only son of George Carter, a successful grain merchant in St. Marys – steep gable roofs, tall windows and chimneys with decorative brickwork

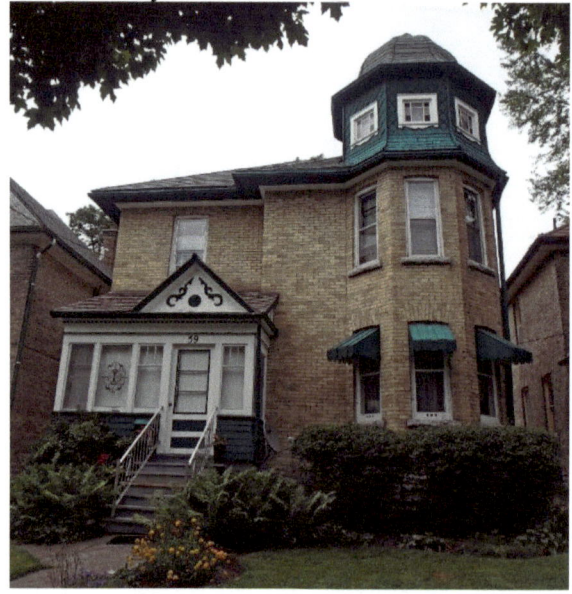

St. Marys Book 4 - 59 Wellington Street South – three-storey capped turret

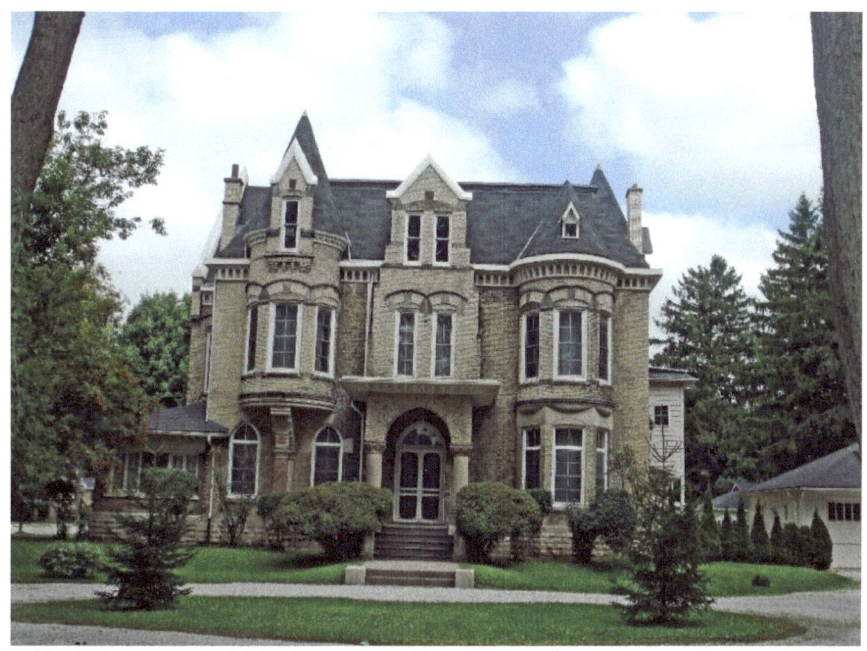

St. Thomas – 1 Wellington Street, St. Thomas – built 1878 (McLachlin House) - turrets, scroll work, bracketing, dormers

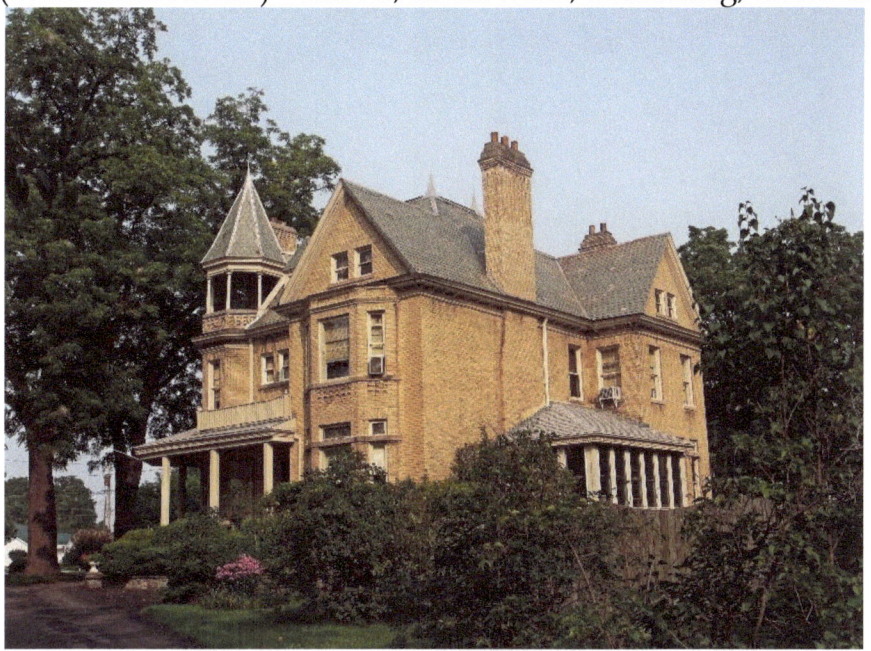

Strathroy - 7 Kittridge Avenue West – Queen Anne - turret

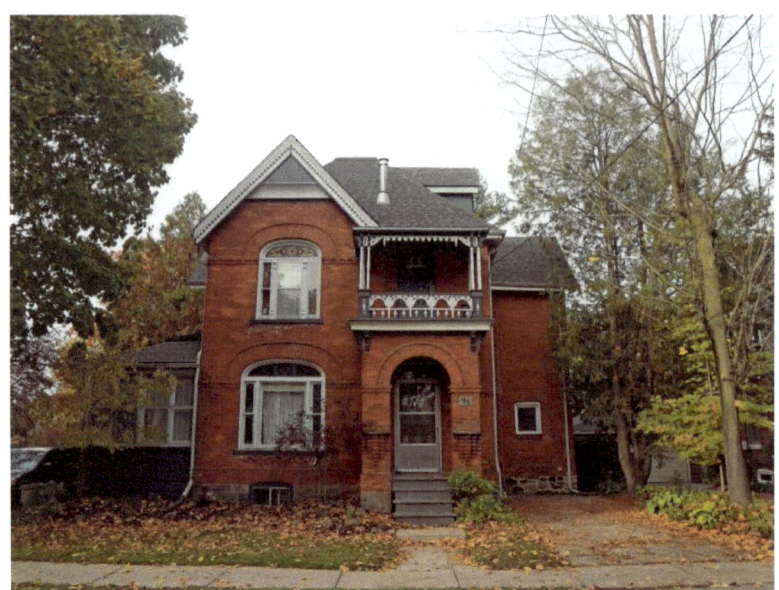

Stouffville - 96 Church Street – c. 1890 – Romanesque/Queen Anne – built by Nathan Forsyth as his residence, local master builder - corbelled brick string course, balcony over verandah

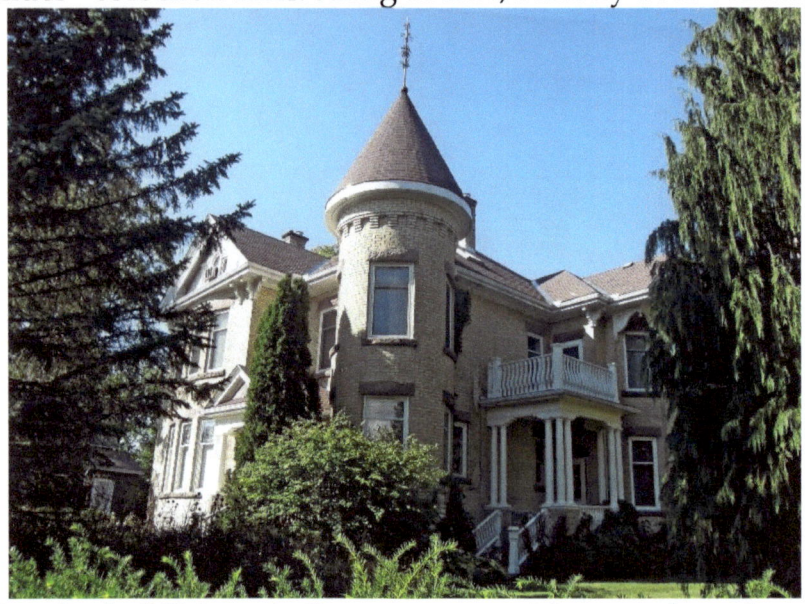

Stratford - 2 Britannia Street - turret with cone-shaped cap, Palladian window in gable, cornice brackets

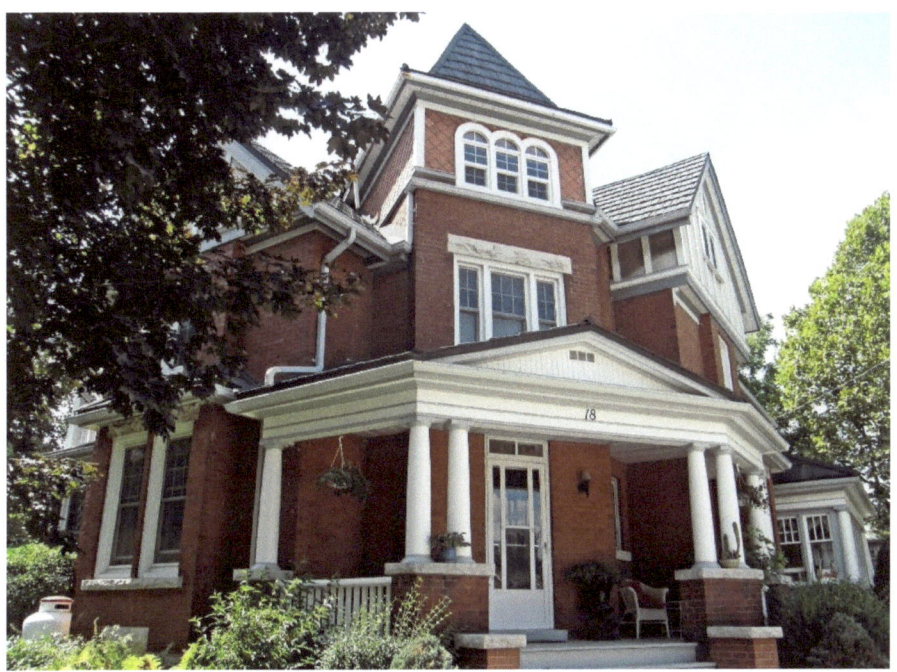

Tavistock - #18 – Queen Anne style – three-story tower, Doric pillars supporting veranda with pediment

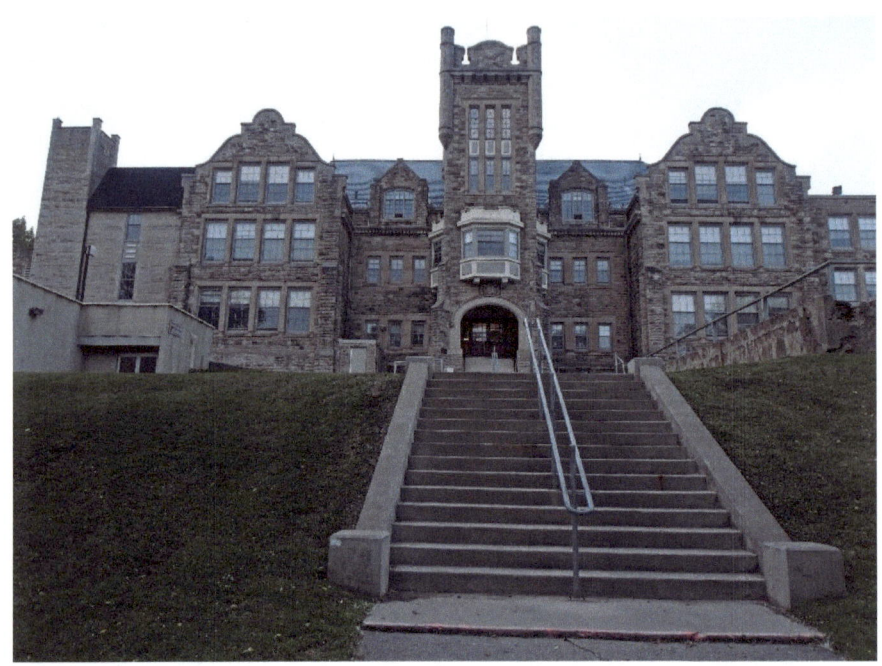

Thunder Bay (Port Arthur Book 1) - 401 Red River Road – Port Arthur Collegiate Institute was constructed in 1909 of Simpson Island stone. Due to decreasing enrollment, the school was closed in 2007. Lakehead University purchased the building and it is now the Bora Laskin Faculty of Law.

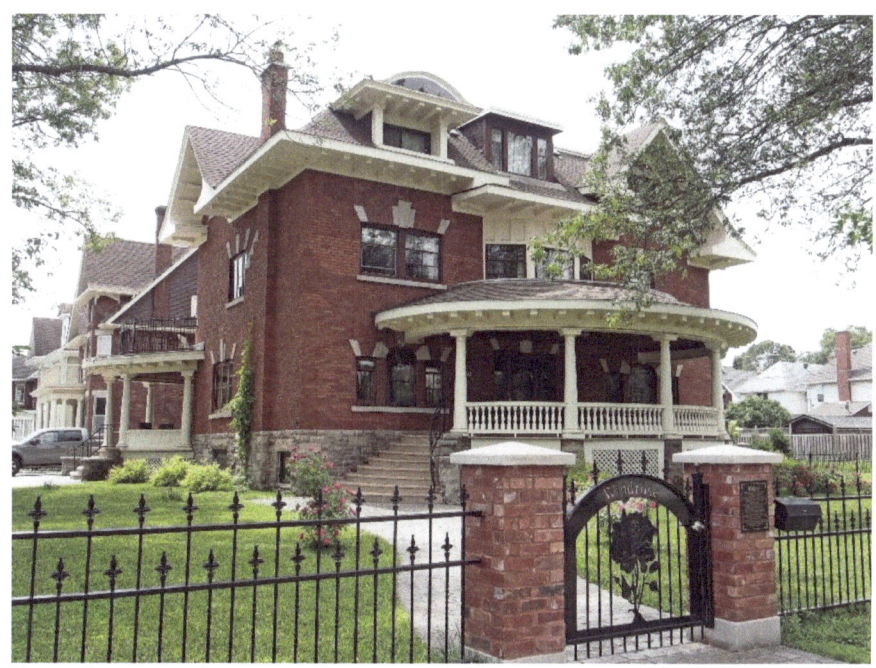

Thunder Bay (Fort William Book 1) - 1100 Ridgeway Street East – Windrose was built in 1910 for Frederick and Cora Morris – he was a solicitor in Fort William beginning in 1897. Queen Anne Revival style – red brick contrasted with cut stone, wood and a rubble stone coursed foundation. The front façade is asymmetrical and the roofline is irregular. The central bay is flat topped, another bay has a rounded dormer, and the third bay has a pointed dormer. The façade has two Palladian windows on the first floor, and a second-floor bay window which suit the Queen Anne style. The house has two rounded verandas supported by classically inspired columns.

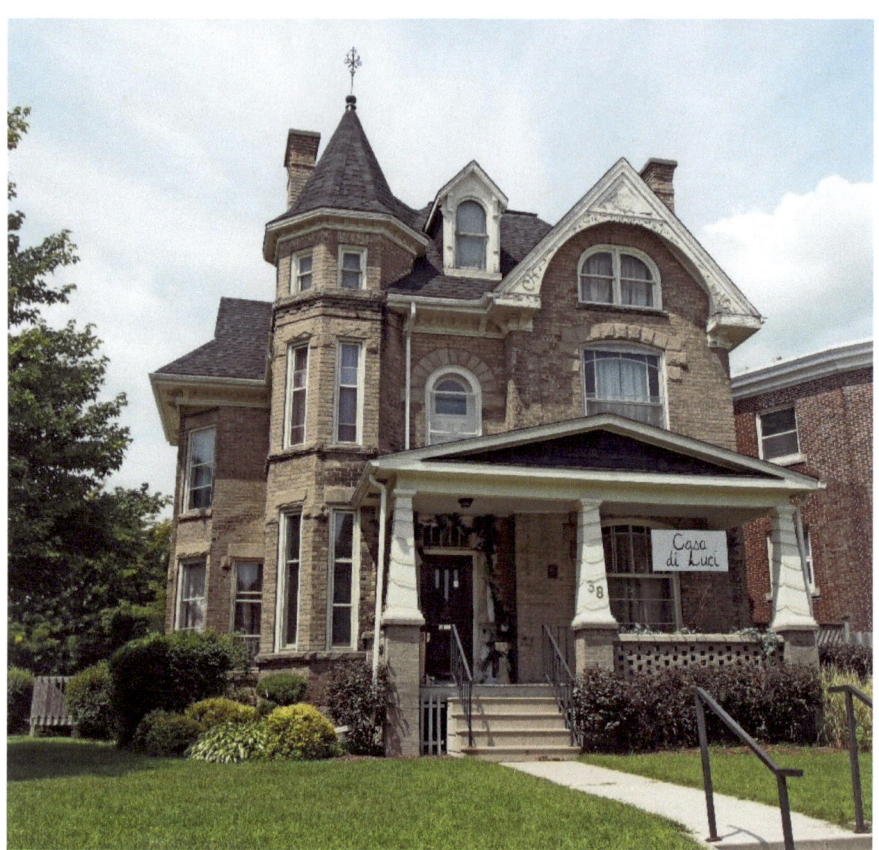

Tillsonburg - 38 Ridout Street West - Casa di Luca Restaurant - This two and a half storey house was built in 1870 as the manse for the adjacent United Church. The front façade has gingerbread in the gable, small dentil trim under the eaves, and rough stone window surrounds; two-storey turret with a cone-shaped roof.

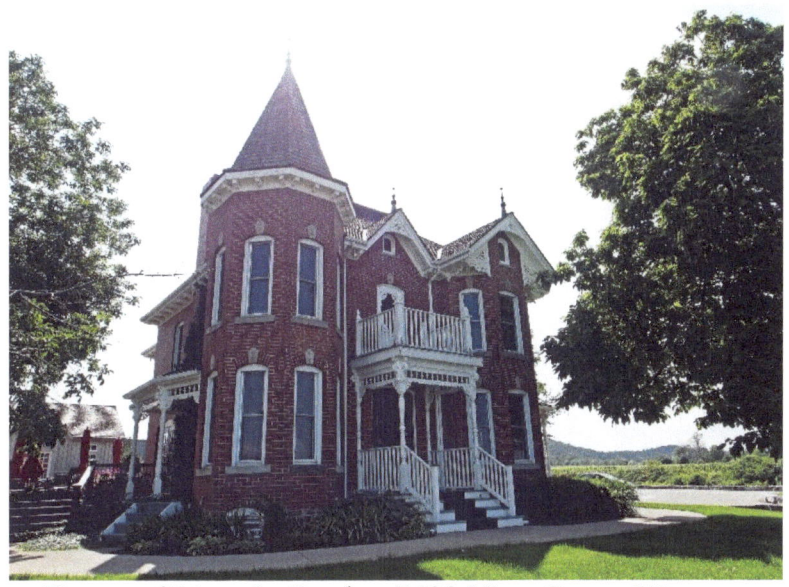

Town of Lincoln Book – 5600 King Street West, Beamsville – The property was a Crown Grant of 52 acres to a loyalist from New Jersey named William W. Kitchen around 1790. He married Alice Beam and they had nine children. William and Alice's youngest son, Jacob married Jane Dennis. Their only son, William Dennis Kitchen married Margaret Henry and built the house in 1885 on the bench of the escarpment, just west of the Thirty Mile Creek. The house was built with red bricks. The turret has square and rounded cedar shingles, topped with a finial. There are two tall corbeled chimneys, and a hipped roof with a flat belvedere. The gables have carved fretwork brackets and barge board. The tall bay windows are topped with segmental arches and decorative keystones. The front porch has an overhead balcony, and like the side porches, features turned posts, balustrades, spandrels and brackets. From 1999 to 2009, the house was owned and restored by Norman and Sherry Beal, who transformed the property into an estate winery. In 2009 Wendy Midgley and her husband Chef Ross Midgley purchased the Kitchen House and the Coach House from the Beals.

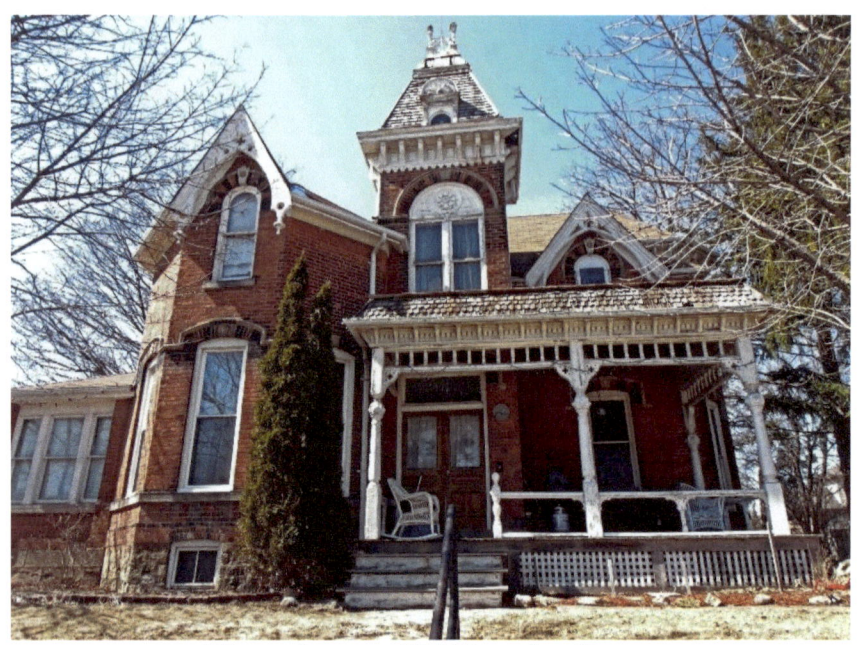
Waterdown - 289 Dundas Street

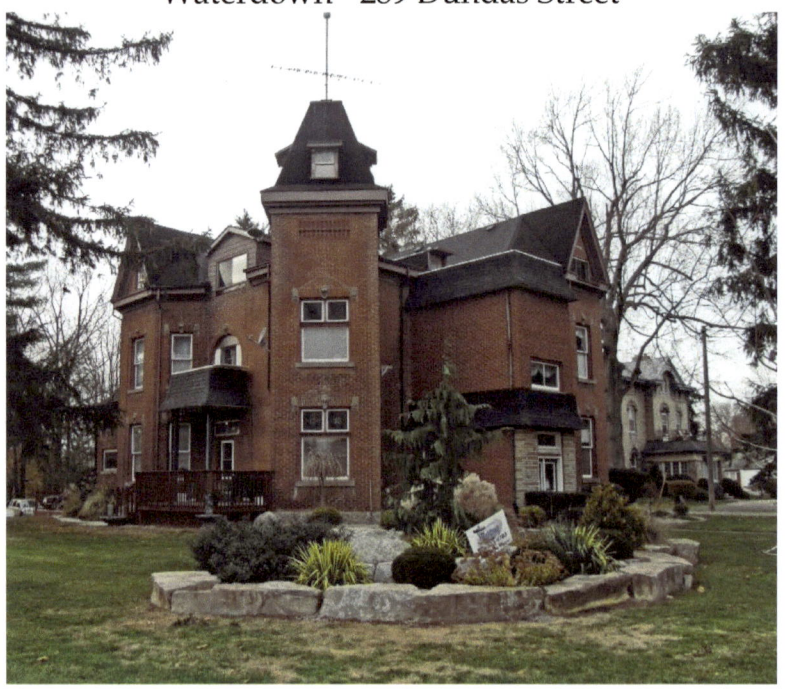
Waterford - 3½ story tower

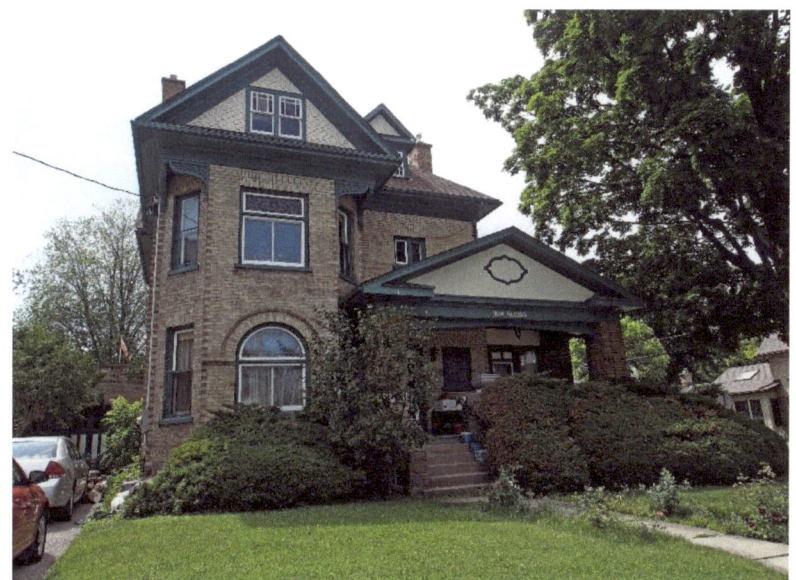

Waterloo Book 1 - 61 Dorset Street – "Bon Accord" – Victorian Queen Anne style built in 1898, stained glass windows, Romanesque style window arches on ground floor windows

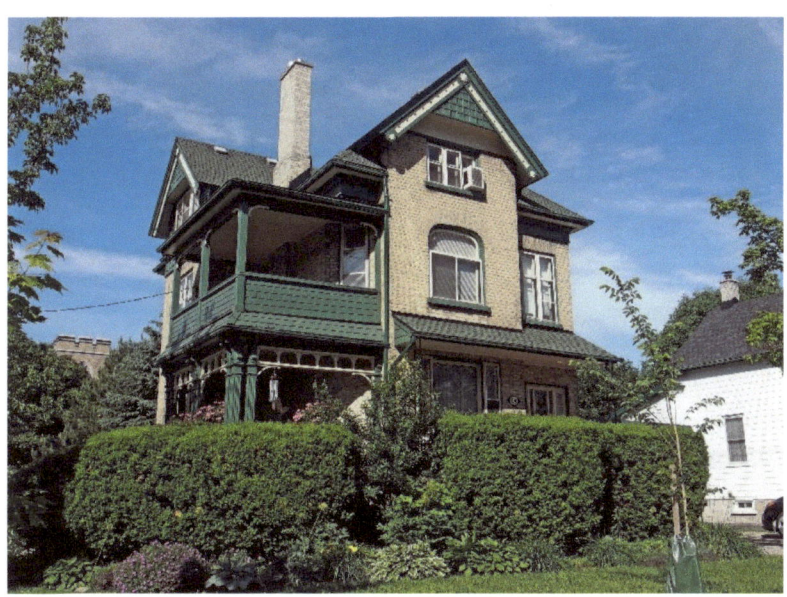

Waterloo Book 2 - 190 Mary Street – two-story verandah

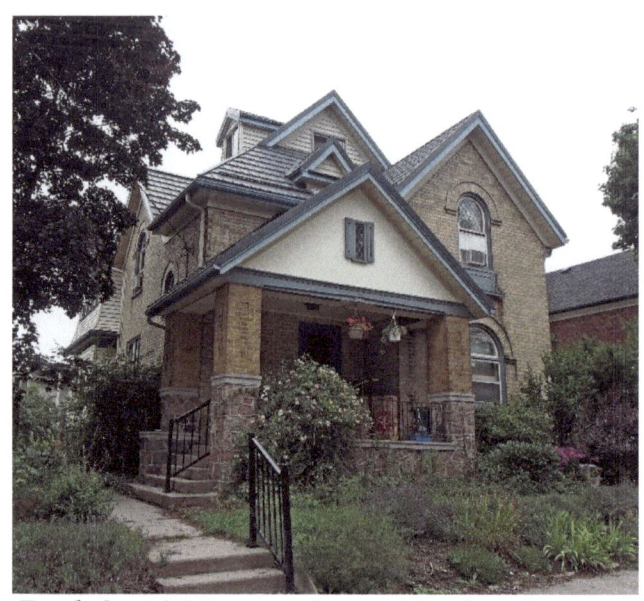

Waterloo Book 3 - 107 Regina Street North – Queen Anne Vernacular, round window voussoirs

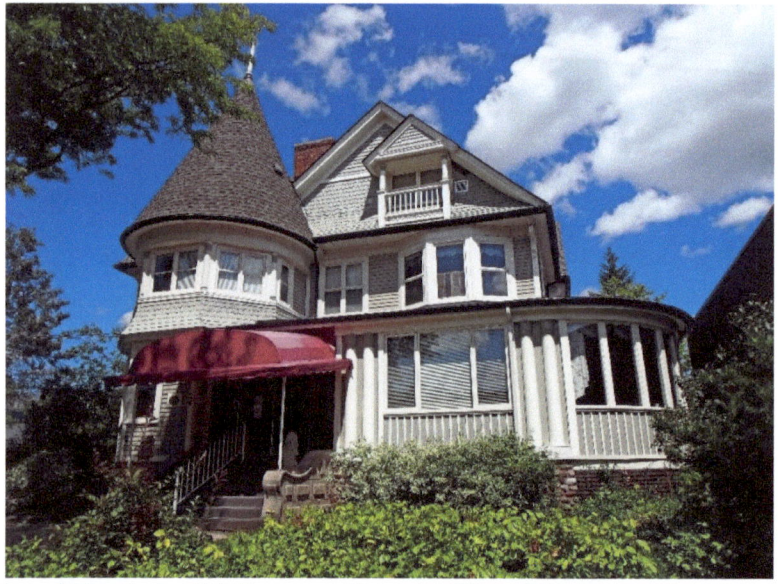

Welland Book 1 - 24 Burgar Street – The Glasgow-Fortner House – 1859 – now Rinderlins Dining Rooms

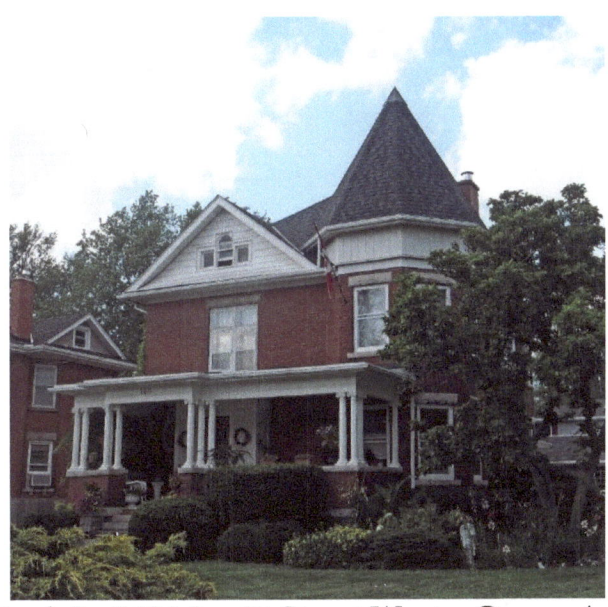

Welland Book 2 - 160 Merritt Street West – Queen Anne style – turret, Palladian window in gable, Ionic capitals on pillared verandah

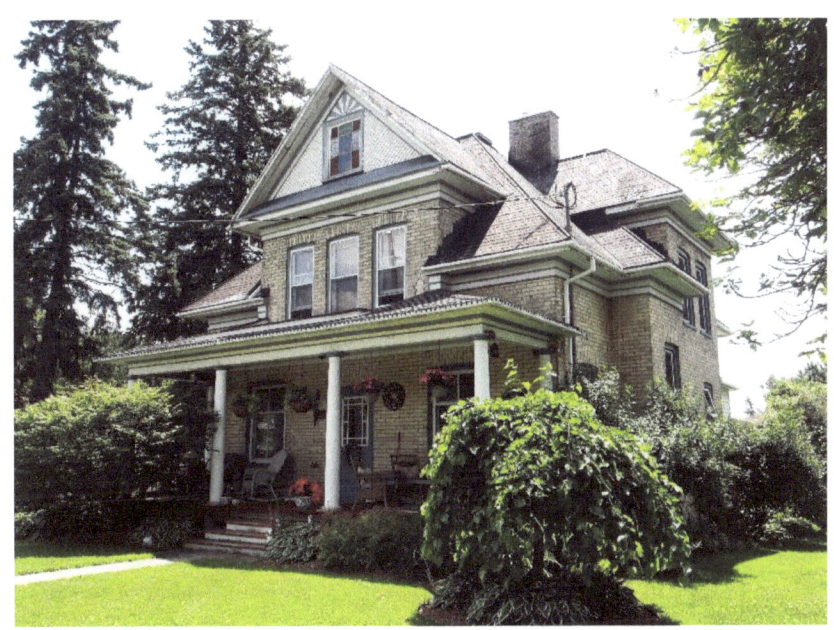

Wellesley - 1110 Queen's Bush Road

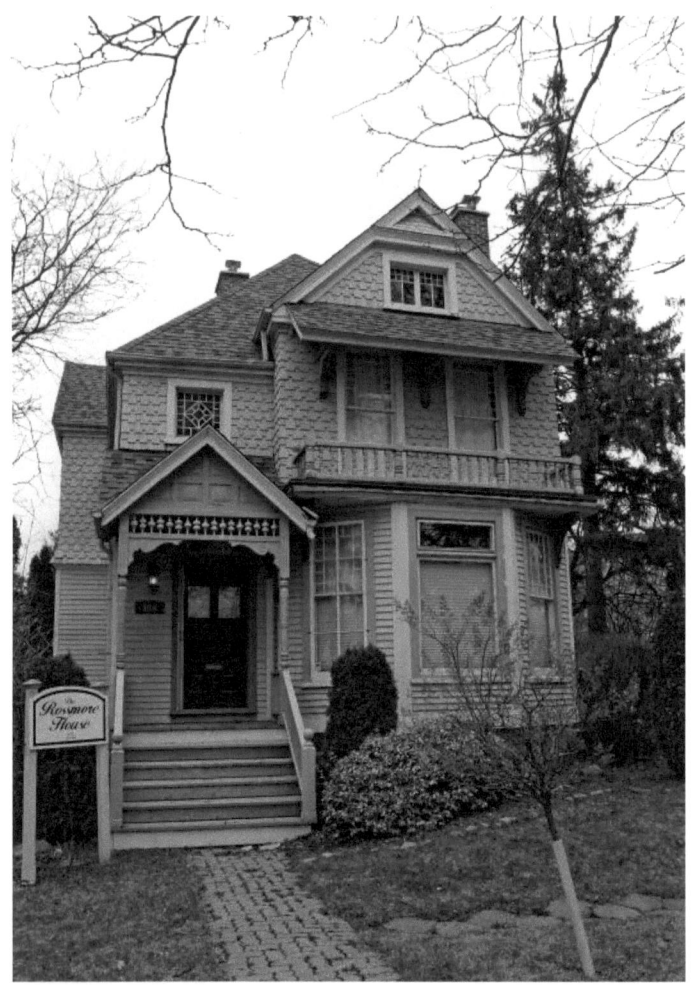

Whitby Book 1 - 404 Dunlop Street West – c. 1888-89 – Queen Anne Revival style – asymmetrical design – built for George Ross – Mrs. Ross was president of Whitby Women's Institute and founder of the Victorian Order of Nurses in Ontario County.

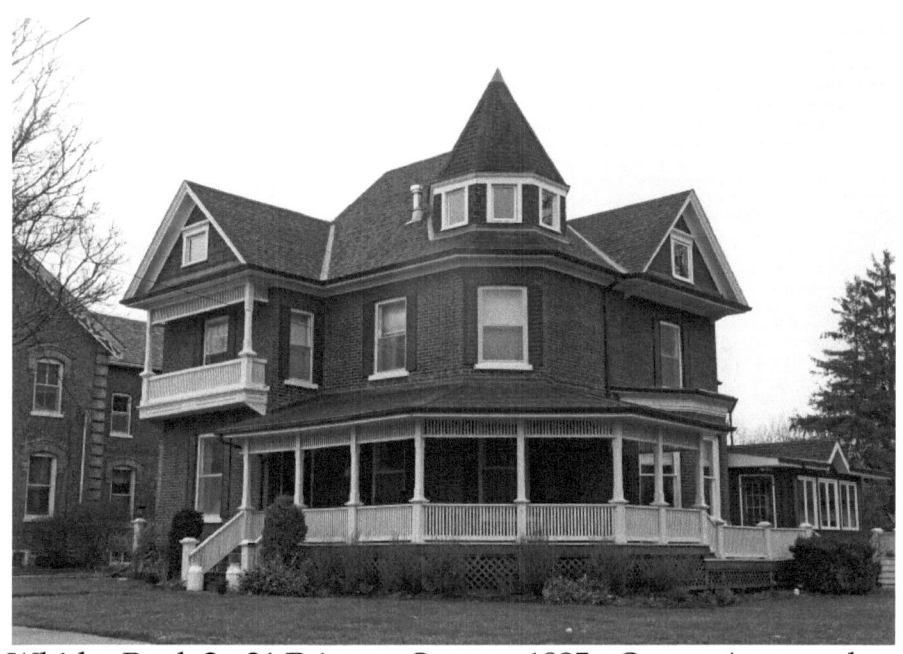

Whitby Book 2 - 21 Princess Street – 1895 - Queen Anne style, engaged tower, chevron pattern shingles on west gable and basket weave pattern on the tower, balcony and verandah wooden railings

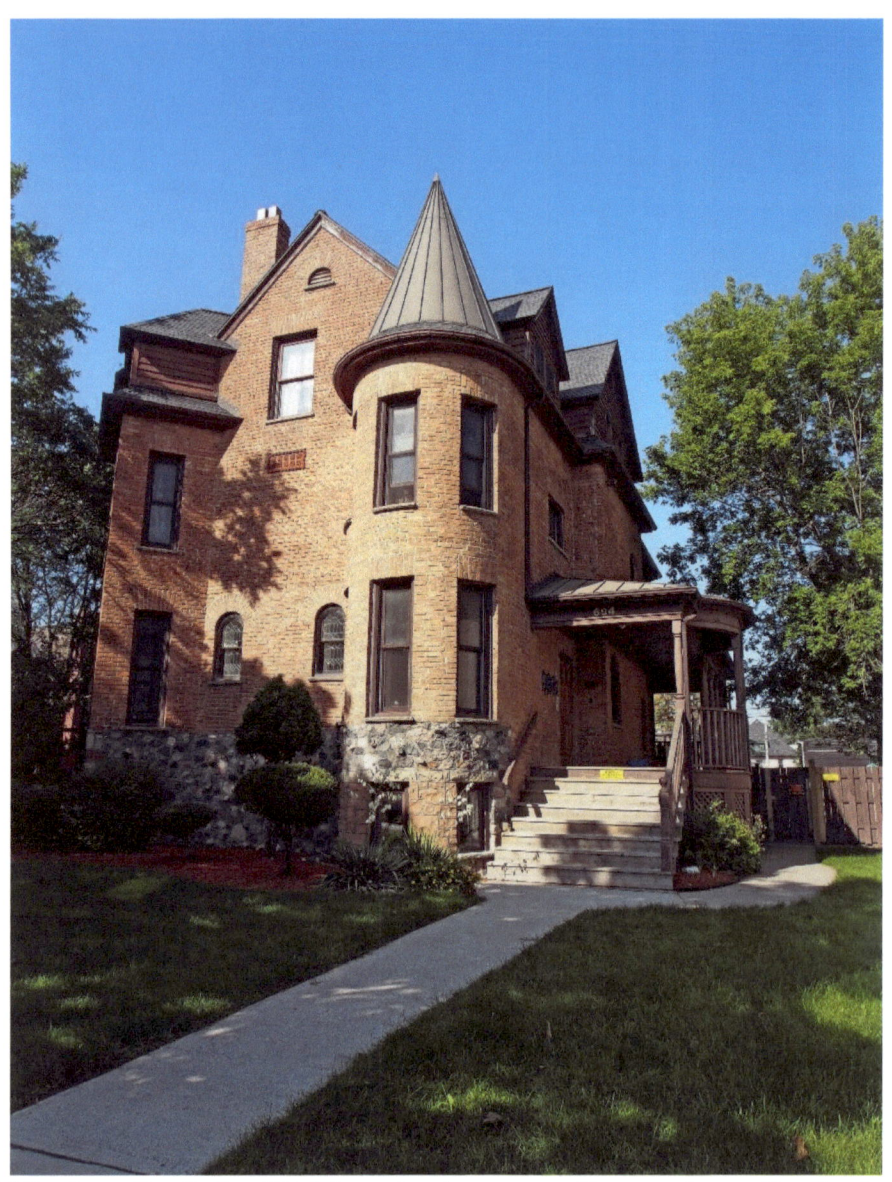

Windsor Book 2 - 694 Victoria Avenue - Queen Anne Revival style with Romanesque influence, 1890-95; cone-capped turret, cyclopean stone detail (stone construction marked by the use of large irregular blocks without mortar), ornamental terra cotta inset

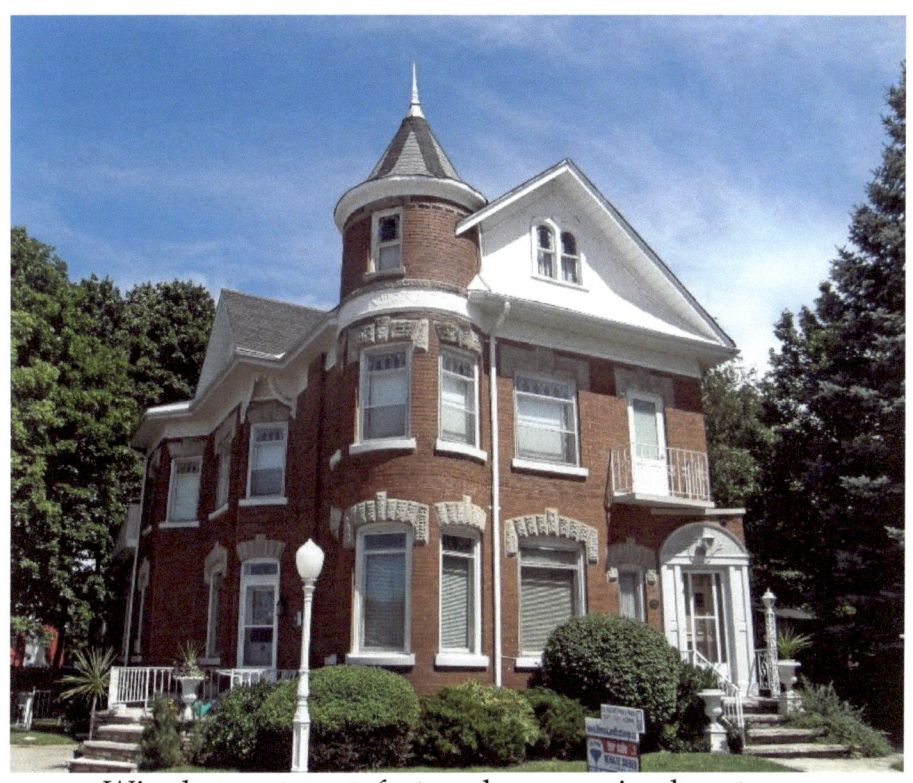

Wingham – turret, fretwork, voussoirs, keystones

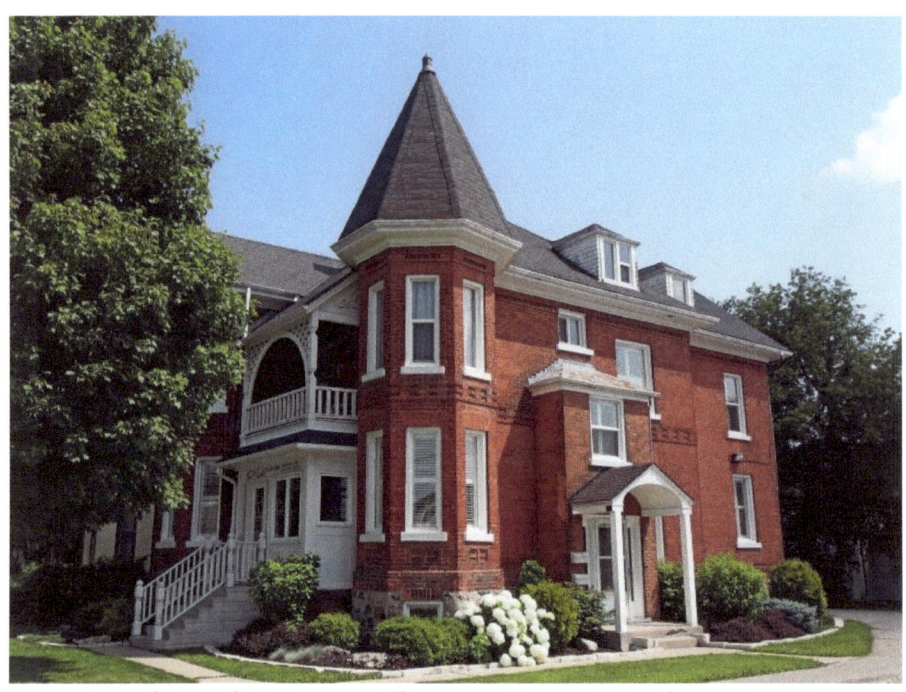

Woodstock Book 2 - 36 Wellington Street North – c. 1854 - Queen Anne – full two-story with attic, red brick, gable roof, two hip roofs with dormers, two-story bay window with gable roof, vergeboard with pendant posts and large brackets, porch and balcony have turned posts, spindles, lattice and bric-a-brac, string course is patterned brickwork, six-sided two-story tower with steep hip roof topped with finial, paired post support gable roof side porch

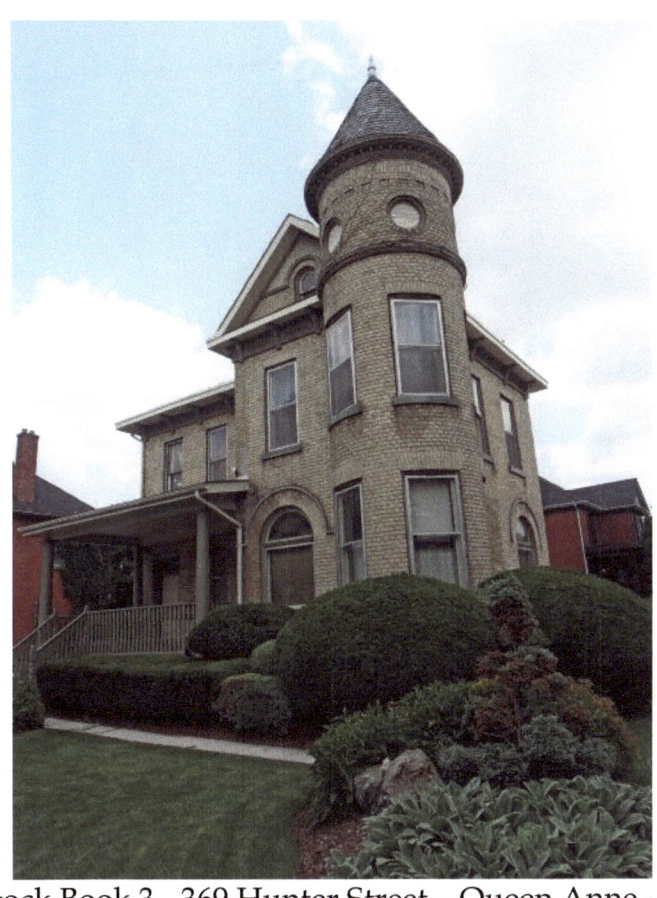

Woodstock Book 3 - 369 Hunter Street – Queen Anne – 2½ storey turret, Romanesque style window voussoirs, cornice brackets

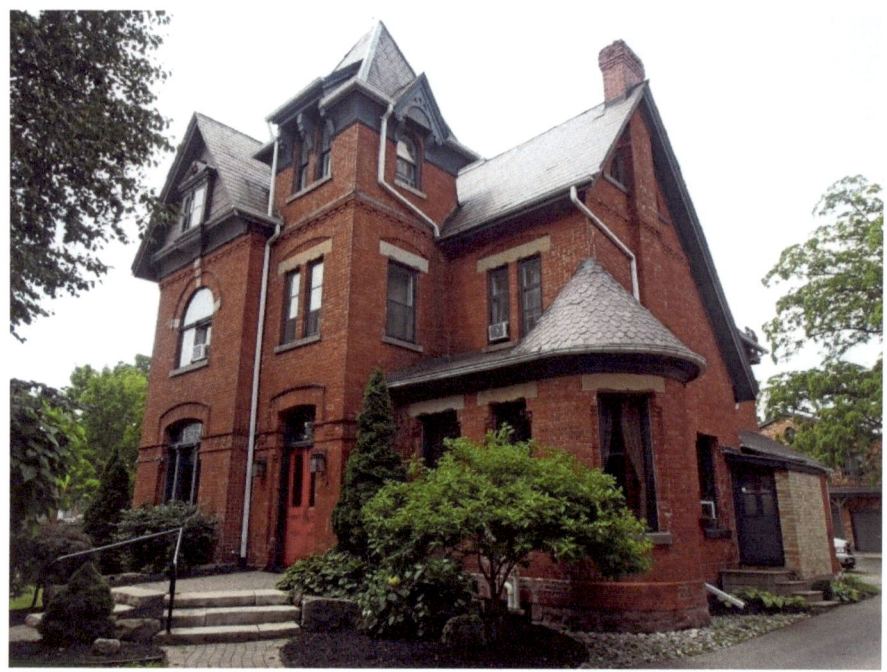

Woodstock Book 4 - 33 Light Street – c. 1869 - Queen Anne - two story with attic, red brick, slate roof with fish scale slate on towers, gable roof, styled stone lintel, keystone and drip course above windows and doorways, corbel cornice encircle the house at the eaves, dormer casement window in gable has pediment lintel, paired windows in square tower and wall dormer, square tower has steep hip roof, circular tower has cone roof, double door topped with segmental transom

Other Books by Barbara Raue

Coins of Gold
Arrows, Indians and Love
The Life and Times of Barbara
The Cromwell Family Book
Laura Secord Discovered
Daddy Where Are You?

Montana Series
Book 1: Montana Dream
Book 2: Life on the Montana Frontier
Book 3: Montana to Boston and Back
Book 4: Montana Sons Go to War
Book 5: Montana Sons Return from War

Book 1: Rite of Passage
Book 2: Rite of Marriage

© 2019 by Barbara Raue - All the photos in this book have been taken with my cameras. I own the rights to them.

Barbara is The Authority on Saving Our History One Photo at a Time. She is pursuing her interest in photography and architecture by preserving a record through photos of old buildings from the 1800s and 1900s with their unique architecture. Enjoy the beautiful architecture in the comfort of your living room. Dream about what it was like in those bygone days. Dream about what it was like to live in a mansion like one of those in this book.

Barbara Raue, a wife, mother and grandmother, is an avid reader and writer. She has researched and compiled several family histories. In 2010, Barbara published her book "Coins of Gold," which celebrates the courageous life of her mother, May Todd. Barbara's second book is a historical fiction "Arrows, Indians and Love" which takes place in Boonesborough, Kentucky during the time of Daniel Boone. In 2013, Barbara published *The Cromwell Family Book* in which she traces her ancestry generations back into Great Britain. Her second novel is called *Laura Secord Discovered,* in which the story of Laura's service during the War of 1812 is shared. Barbara's memoir is titled *Daddy Where Are You?* It tells of her life growing up without a father. Five novels in the Montana Series have been published, *Montana Dream, Life on the Montana Frontier, Montana to Boston and Back, Montana Sons Go to War*, and *Montana Sons Return from War*.

This is a link to Barbara's website to view all of her books
http://barbararaue.ca

www.ingramcontent.com/pod-product-compliance
Lightning Source LLC
Chambersburg PA
CBHW040226220526
45473CB00001B/135